D1795545

The
SALES
ACCELERATOR

How to expand your sales capability to
compete successfully *in any market*

YAMINI VIRANI

RETHINK PRESS

First published in Great Britain in 2019 by Rethink Press (www.rethinkpress.com)

© Copyright Yamini Virani

All rights reserved. No part of this publication may be reproduced, stored in or introduced into a retrieval system, or transmitted, in any form, or by any means (electronic, mechanical, photocopying, recording or otherwise) without the prior written permission of the publisher.

The right of Yamini Virani to be identified as the author of this work has been asserted by her in accordance with the Copyright, Designs and Patents Act 1988.

This book is sold subject to the condition that it shall not, by way of trade or otherwise, be lent, resold, hired out, or otherwise circulated without the publisher's prior consent in any form of binding or cover other than that in which it is published and without a similar condition including this condition being imposed on the subsequent purchaser.

Cover image © Shutterstock | redstone

To my parents, Prem and Hargovind Pant

Contents

Introduction

In 2013, I opened a division of my sales consulting practice in Kenya and started working with many Western companies that had subsidiaries here and were looking to grow their presence in Africa. The country directors/country managers or CEOs of those companies were some of the sharpest, most knowledgeable businesspeople in the world and had many years of great experience, with solid backgrounds in finance, operations and marketing. In spite of their diverse résumés, these talented people all had one thing in common: as international executives, they were tasked with meeting huge targets in a market that was, culturally, very different from anything they had experienced elsewhere.

I started to notice that the difference in cultural expectations, compounded by never having been in a sales position before, resulted in a critical disconnect between these CEOs and their sales teams. There was a wide gulf between the strategies created in their companies' boardrooms vs. what was actually being implemented on the ground—which was only made worse by the pressure they felt from their corporate head office and board to produce results. Some of the challenges that CEOs shared with me included:

> "We have aggressive goals to meet, and we need our sales leaders and teams to perform at a higher level, to meet their targets."

> "Our senior executive team needs to be better aligned to our strategy and to execute their plans."

> "Marketing and sales need to work together as a team to achieve sales. We can't have the silo, or 'do it alone', mentality between these departments, or between any other departments for that matter."

> "Sales leaders need to take charge of their teams and be more proactive about driving results."

> "The sales team must deliver on expectations. We need to make sales more consistent, and there has to be a process."

"We have given our teams goals and they are trained in the product, but they still can't meet their targets."

"I want the sales team to step up their game, take more responsibility and be more professional."

"We can't seem to find the right people. We need to hire quickly and train them to sell as fast as we can."

"We spend a lot of money on our brand image and marketing, but I don't feel confident that our sales reps are conveying the right message to our customers."

One day, James, one of my clients and the country director of the largest real estate developer in Africa, asked me the big question: "What do we need to do as leaders to improve our sales performance?"

At the time, I had been working with James' sales team for six months. As a result of our collaboration, his company had already beaten their yearly sales targets for one of their largest products, halfway through the year. He knew this was my area of expertise, and he went on to ask, "Could you come and talk to our executive team at our annual management retreat to discuss what we need to address within our organization to drive sales performance?"

Interestingly, I encountered similar questions from CEOs and senior executives of companies, both in the USA and on the African continent, that were between the US$100–300 million revenue mark.

James's question, along with the challenges I kept hearing from other CEOs I worked with, became the inspiration to write this book and to share my insights on how to transform sales in your organization.

Before I go any further, let me answer the question, you might be asking: "What's your background and experience on sales growth, anyway?"

Selling is not optional

Over the last thirteen years, I have worked with leaders of companies in both the USA and across the African continent to help them beat their sales targets, but my journey into sales was not something I planned. I was trained as a certified public accountant, went to graduate school to get a Master's degree in Business Administration and Finance, and worked in corporate finance and marketing designing financial models for forecasts and evaluating pricing strategies for new products. Then the entrepreneurial bug bit, and in 2006, alongside two other women, I started a management consulting practice in Atlanta, Georgia.

My role in our practice was primarily to consult with clients and offer my expertise. I unequivocally told my partners that I would not be looking for clients, and really, sales was not my cup of tea.

Honestly, I looked down upon selling. As most partnerships do, ours fell apart and I was left holding the bag—and tied to the loan I had taken against my house. Like most professionals I was of the opinion that if I was technically competent in what I did, had the degrees to prove it, and offered a great service, it stood to reason that people would automatically line up for my services, right?

Obviously, that didn't happen. I had no choice but to learn how to sell to get business in the door.

The first three years were tough, to say the least, and I religiously made all the sales mistakes there were to make (after all, I was an overachiever, and I was going to ace this). As a process-driven consultant, I made the habit of analyzing what I did wrong and figuring out a new way. In the early days, while I was good at helping my clients analyze and develop their business strategies, the biggest impact came when I started translating their sales strategies into implementation plans from the perspective of the sales reps in the field and in the context of the organization as a whole.

Most of my clients in those days were running fairly large businesses as CEOs of their companies but had no direct experience of selling to a customer. I, on the other hand, had not only to create a sales strategy for my business, but also to sell directly. Nothing exposes the gaps in your strategy like getting in front of a client to sell your services.

Perspective gaps

In most organizations, there is a constant battle over sales goals. A recurring trend is the gap between the goals the CEO has in mind, and what the sales teams think is realistic, resulting in mistrust on both sides because the interpretation of strategy and expectations don't match.

I recall a meeting I was having with the executive team about a new service line we wanted to introduce in the business. We had conducted market surveys, identified our target markets, and worked out the projected return on investment. We had invested a lot of time and done our homework. From our analysis and sales projections, we would start making money in six months.

It was at this point that I asked the team to consider whether the sales goals we had set would actually get implemented. If we couldn't change the goals, what resources would need to be considered? Could the existing team take on a new service and market without diverting their attention from their existing prospects and clients? By getting the executive team to put themselves in the shoes of their sales managers and reps, they were able to identify beforehand the challenges the salespeople would have to deal with in the implementation and how we could address those beforehand in the launch to ensure targets were met.

At the end of the meeting Mike, the sales director, came over and said, "I am glad you brought that up. I don't think I could have sold my team on the targets alone without having a plan to achieve them."

Interestingly, the CEO said, "It was important to look at a different approach and work together as a team to deal with the challenges now instead of waiting to find out why we hadn't succeeded six months later."

I started working with sales managers and their teams to help them clearly understand sales strategies from the point of view of the executive team and then translate it in terms of what they did on a day-to-day basis. I also trained them in selling techniques to hit their numbers.

At the same time, I worked with the executive team to look at things from the sales reps' perspectives and get an insight into what the market was saying and what stood in the way of us selling our products effectively.

By getting both parties to be able to see things from a different perspective, we started bridging the gap in sales targets and tackled the issues on both fronts. My clients started getting more value from hiring me because I brought two perspectives to the table. And since I had made many of the potential mistakes, I used the lessons of what not to do to save my clients money, time and heartache, by preventing them from making those mistakes in the first place.

Change your perspective, change your sales

As a senior leader of your company, perhaps you are in charge of launching a new division of your company in Africa or elsewhere. Or perhaps you are growing your company to be the market leader, through aggressive targets or claiming the first-mover advantage. Whatever the case, you obviously have immense experience and expertise in your field, and it is not a matter of chance that you find yourself in this position of leadership.

It is not my place to tell you what you should or should not be doing. Nor is this book about dealing with cultural issues or how to do business in Africa—or, for that matter, in the USA. I have consciously steered away from this because I believe that we cannot make generalized statements about how to work within any one culture. If we did then we would blind ourselves to opportunities that exist around us, fall into the trap of blaming cultural differences for issues and miss the opportunity for creative problem-solving. I believe instead that the best way to deal with any situation in any culture is to focus on your own perspective, be willing to challenge it and approach the issue from multiple perspectives to find the best solution. The focus of this book is on solving sales problems creatively and expanding your leadership capacity for change. I have tried to share case studies and examples from companies in both the USA and Africa to illustrate how these principles operate universally.

I invite you to expand into different perspectives and ask a different question of yourself: "Is there another perspective that I might not be seeing?"

Changing your perspective changes your interpretations—in other words, changing the perspective changes the stories we tell ourselves. Whether you have been in sales before, or not, doesn't matter. When you start looking at situations and sales from a different perspective, you will find multiple angles and, as a result, solutions that you may not have previously considered.

By sharing my own experiences and those of other leaders in positions similar to yours, I endeavor to spark a thought process around sales that looks beyond the obvious and creates the opportunity for meaningful conversations with your teams for long-term sales performance and growth. My intent is that you will find insights on how to drive sales performance as you look at how the Sales Accelerator Model takes a 360-degree approach to sales and positions an organization for long-term sustainable sales growth.

1

The Sales Accelerator Model

"What should we be doing with our competition?" the email read. I received this in response to a brief questionnaire I sent out to a group of senior executives for a strategy session I was going to facilitate. I wanted to get their questions and insights on the areas that were impacting sales growth and performance.

This particular email piqued my interest because when we think of sales growth, our tendency is to look outward and see what the competition is doing and how we might compare, especially as we're expanding into new markets. And, yes, it's important to keep your eye on the market, stay on top of developments to understand how they impact your sales, and make the required adjustments to your product, pricing or strategy. But the perception that the road to sales growth lies outside can be misleading and take you down a circuitous path.

Your competitive advantage in your market does not necessarily need to come from your product or service. Instead, it could come from a highly engaged sales team that is focused on delivering and communicating value to your customers. Leading companies in pursuit of sales growth understand that driving sales performance is about focusing on the internal growth factors as much as it is about focusing on the external ones.

All too often, the potential for massive growth may lie within but gets overlooked because familiarity with the status quo can blindside us to the opportunities. The Sales Accelerator unearths the untapped potential for sales success by focusing the lens on five critical internal growth factors for driving sales performance.

The five internal growth factors

What are these five key internal growth factors and how can the Sales Accelerator Model help you set the foundation for sustainable sales?

Think of it like building a car. You need the engine, the frame and chassis, the braking system, and the transmission all working in sync, along with the necessary wiring to connect them all together, before you can rev up and compete against the other cars in the Safari Rally or NASCAR Cup. Running your sales machine is very much like that. There are five key components that need to be in place to enable you to complete a successful stage or lap every single time, compete successfully, and win the race.

The Sales Accelerator Model

Just having one component alone will not work; each needs to be supported by the others for optimum performance. Investing in sales or product training alone, or hiring a good sales manager without a sales performance management team, cannot work in isolation to improve sales performance and achieve the success you desire.

Having worked with hundreds of companies over the last thirteen years, I've learned that creating an environment for long-term, sustainable sales performance depends on a company being able to implement all of the five internal growth factors for sales success.

The book is organized around these five internal growth factors of the Sales Accelerator Model, and looks at how you can set the foundation for sustainable sales in your organization. Each component is designed to address common performance issues that put the brakes on sales growth and how to resolve these issues so that you can gear up for sales acceleration. As you explore each factor in more depth, you will find practical ideas on how you can use it in your organization and also learn what other companies have done to solve common challenges and grow their revenues.

Below you will find a brief description of each factor, its purpose and a preview of what it can do for you.

Factor #1: Strategy alignment—align goals at all levels

Ensure that the sales strategy you develop in your boardroom is exactly what is implemented on the front lines. I want to draw your attention to three key areas that are critical for the successful implementation of your sales strategy:

1) Make your strategy relatable

In order to bring in consistent sales results, your sales strategy must be relatable and understood at all levels among the senior leadership team, middle management and at the front lines.

Quick preview:

- Identify the five common blind spots that prevent leaders from seeing the internal challenges to sales growth

- Align your boardroom strategy with your front-line action

- Understand how your middle management can translate the overarching sales strategy into daily execution

- Understand how to set goals that motivate your team and why stretch goals could work against you

- Visit www.celebrusstrategies.com and use the Sales Calculator to see if you will meet your goals for the month and, even more importantly, how your strategy translates and appears from the perspective of your sales reps

2) Align your sales process with how your customers like to buy

Ensure that the steps and actions that your sales teams take align with a prospect to enable them to make a buying decision.

Quick preview:

- Take the Sales Process Questionnaire in Chapter 3 to find out for yourself if your sales process is supporting or hindering the ability to close sales

- Find out how an effective sales process can prevent the eight leaks in your revenue pipeline

- Identify eight ways you can redesign and improve your sales process for better conversion rates and buyer engagement

- Understand how to gain better visibility and control over your pipeline.

3) Align your marketing and sales for revenue growth

Whether you're launching a new product or selling an existing product, marketing and sales collaboration and alignment is critical to your revenue growth.

Quick preview:

- Understand the common challenges that prevent your marketing investment from turning into sales revenue and what to do about them

- Determine which of the seven strategies you will use to align sales and marketing for revenue growth for your company

- Understand how to keep the focus on the customer with a consistent value proposition

- Know how to spot opportunities for success as you evaluate your marketing initiatives

Factor #2: Savvy sales force—recruit the best

When services or products from competitors are similar or even identical to yours, the engagement and trust your sales force create with your customers will be the differentiators. This section focuses on how you can turn your sales force and sales leadership into your competitive advantage.

Quick preview:

- Identify the six key competencies and skills needed in your sales manager before you make a decision about whom to hire

- Understand that your sales manager is a key implementer of your sales strategy and how to get your managers to proactively drive sales instead of playing catch up

- Know how to identify the skills, behaviors and knowledge that are required for high performance in a particular sales role

- Use our unique approach to hire a high-potential sales team, onboard new recruits to quickly meet sales targets and bring out the best in them

Factor #3: Sales agility—train for performance

Sales agility—or how fast one learns and applies new skills and adapts to changing situations—is the new currency for sales success in sales leaders and salespeople. Your customers' needs are constantly changing, there is more competition than ever before in the marketplace and instant gratification is an expectation. Your customers don't need salespeople; they need experts who will partner with them in the buying process, make sense of the data and empower them to make the right decision.

Quick preview:

- Understand how to embed a culture of learning into your everyday routine

- Understand how to align your training with your sales strategy and focus on solving real-life problems that reps face in the marketplace

- Know how to deliver a phenomenal sales experience

- Identify eleven strategies to proactively and systematically increase your referrals and get more repeat business

Factor #4: Sales coaching—coach for business impact

Coaching has the ability to transform your sales leaders and teams, and to become the differentiating factor between your sales performance and your competitors. Coaching for performance is no longer a "nicety" but a critical component for maximizing the effectiveness of team members in closing new accounts more quickly, becoming apt problem-solvers and achieving their sales targets.

Quick preview:

- Understand how coaching can help your managers meet their quotas

- Understand how your reps can overcome obstacles that hold them back from maximizing performance and become more resourceful

- Manage performance issues and create a culture of problem-solving and coaching for high performance

- Understand how to align reward systems with your team's intrinsic motivation

- Identify five keys to creating a culture that supports your strategic initiatives

Factor #5: Sales Scorecard—measure and monitor results

Without a dashboard it's impossible to tell if you're on track to win. Regular reporting is a key ingredient of successful sales performance because it keeps the focus on four fundamental questions:

- Where are we in relation to our goals?

- Why are we winning or losing sales?

- What problems or trends need to be addressed?

- What actions should this information lead to/ what should we do differently?

Quick preview:

- Know how to build a reporting structure that is focused on problem-solving and overcomes reluctance to reporting

- Understand why your objectives and purpose should drive your metrics and what metrics should be measured

- Understand how to get the most out of your customer relationship management (CRM)

Embarking on the sales growth journey

Sales success doesn't just depend on the sales rep sticking to their performance routines. Maximizing performance is about having a structure in place that enables peak performance. Sustained sales performance is about having all the key pieces in place and cultivating a healthy alignment between them to reach goals smarter and faster. You will probably find that you already have some or all of these in place. If you want to take a quick assessment of where your organization stands, download the Sales Accelerator Assessment from www.celebrusstrategies.com.

If you're thinking "I already know this," I invite you to ask yourself a different question: "How well are each of these areas working in my organization to create sustained sales performance?" If you think one or more of these areas of your business could use some work, then read on.

FACTOR ONE

STRATEGY ALIGNMENT— ALIGN GOALS AT ALL LEVELS

2
Sales Performance Doesn't Start With The Team—It Starts With You

According to Friedrich Nietzsche, a German philosopher and one of the most influential of all modern thinkers, "We hear only those questions for which we are in a position to find answers."[1] There are many questions that need to be asked outside of our experience.

Asking questions outside of our experience also means being willing to acknowledge that as leaders we all have blind spots that can inhibit us from seeing challenges and opportunities that are present.

The quest for internal change starts with an awareness and recognition of the blind spots that get in the way.

---

1   O'Hara, S (2004) *Nietzsche Within Your Grasp*. Hoboken, NJ: Wiley.

Here we look at the five most common blind spots that prevent leaders from seeing the internal challenges to sales growth, and how to work through them to turn them into opportunities and solutions for your organization.

Check your blind spots

Blind spot #1: The perception dilemma— what vs. how

"I feel that the top management is unrealistic in terms of expectations," confided Jane, the head of HR. "I don't think they see it that way, though. I really do need your help at the retreat to address expectations."

Jane shared her concerns with me during a conversation we were having about the strategic retreat I was going to facilitate for her company, and it wasn't the first time that a head of sales, a VP or an HR leader shared such concerns with me.

At the end of the day, there is always a logical reason for how goals are set by senior management. Whether it is based on an improvement over last year's revenue or revenue targets that investors, banks or shareholders expect the company to meet, senior management is focused on a single question: "What needs to be accomplished?" Hence, their mandate becomes, "We need to achieve x in revenue." It makes perfect sense to cascade the goals to the sales team.

When goals are presented to sales team, however, their primary focus is not on what, but how. The sales team is less concerned with what needs to be accomplished and more focused on the question, "How are we going to achieve this number?"

These are two separate paradigms—variations in perspective. When the "how" doesn't look doable to the sales team, or when there is a lack of understanding of the support they will receive from the top to accomplish the goals that have been mandated, it creates the perception of "unrealistic expectations from above."

The real issue may not be the goals, per se, but the fact that both sides responsible for achieving the targets are looking at it from two completely different angles. Each side has a fixed perspective that makes it hard to understand the other side's point of view.

In Jane's case, when the conversation around sales goals began at the retreat, I knew I had to bridge the perspective gap so that top management could see things from their sales teams' perspective. So I took them through the goal conversion exercise explained over the following pages. This is something you might want to try with your team as well. Beware—don't let the simplicity of the exercise trick you. I am sure you use more detailed versions of this exercise in your company to help you calculate activity levels and conversion rates for your sales teams. For the sake of this exercise, though, I just want you to focus on the big picture.

The goal conversion exercise

You can use the Sales Calculator which is online at www.celebrusstrategies.com to see whether you will meet your monthly goals, or you can walk through this exercise using the following steps. Most importantly, make sure you reflect on and answer the questions after Step 6.

Step 1: Take your annual goal and divide it by 12 months to arrive at a monthly goal

$$\frac{\text{Annual sales goal}}{12} = \text{monthly goal}$$

$$\frac{\text{Example: } \$120,000,000}{12} = 10,000,000 \text{ per month}$$

Step 2: Calculate your average sale price

Average sale price can be calculated as follows:

If you have different price points for a similar product, take an average price. For example, take the last ten sales and divide the value by ten to get an average.

If you have multiple products, you can take sales targets for each product line and work through this exercise. The goal of the exercise is not so much about accuracy of numbers but the ability to see a different perspective.

Step 3: Calculate the number of sales units needed to meet your target

Let's say you sell real estate and each plot sells for $100,000. Take your monthly goal and divide it by the sales price to give you the number of plots you need to sell per month to meet your target.

Monthly goal: $10,000,000

Average sales price: $100,000

$$\frac{\text{Monthly goal}}{\text{average sales price}} = \text{no. of sales units per month}$$

$$= \frac{10,000,000}{100,000}$$

$$= 100 \text{ units}$$

Step 4: Calculate the number of interested prospects needed to meet your monthly goal (divide the number of sales units by your sales team's average conversion rate to find the number of interested sales prospects your team needs per month)

What is the average conversion or closure rate for your sales team? Let's say that for every ten interested prospects, they close two, which equals a (2/10) or 20% conversion rate. We need to find out how many interested prospects your sales team needs every month to be able to hit their sales goals for the month.

$$\frac{\text{No. of sales units}}{\substack{\text{Your team's average} \\ \text{conversion rate } \%}} = \frac{100}{0.20}$$

$$= 500 \text{ interested prospects}$$

Step 5: Calculate the level of activity needed to get these interested prospects

But wait, don't stop there. To get these interested prospects, there is another conversion rate. Let's say your sales team's primary strategy to get leads is through cold calling and in order for them to get one interested prospect they need to make at least ten cold calls or achieve a 10% closure rate (1/10).

So to get 500 interested prospects, they need to contact:

$$\frac{\text{No. of interested prospects}}{\text{Activity conversion rate } \%} = \frac{500}{0.10}$$

$$= 5,000 \text{ contacts}$$

Step 6: Calculate how much this works out to per team member

Let's say you have a team of five sales reps.

That means each rep needs an average of 500/5 or 100 sales conversations with interested prospects to meet their goals.

$$\frac{\text{No. of interested prospects}}{\text{no. of sales reps}} = \frac{500}{5}$$

$$= \frac{100 \text{ interested}}{\text{prospects}}$$

To reach their target, each team member has to contact 5,000

$$\frac{\text{(see Step 5 above)}}{5} = \frac{1,000 \text{ contacts}}{\text{per month}}$$

$$\text{or} \quad \frac{1,000}{20} = 50 \text{ prospects contacted a day}$$

Your goals and activity formula

		Examples	Your numbers
Step 1: Your annual sales goal	$	120,000,000	
Divide by 12 =			
Your monthly goal	$	10,000,000	
Step 2: Your average sales price	$	100,000	
Step 3: No. of sales units to meet goal (monthly goal / average sale price)		100	
Your team's average conversion rate (from interested prospect to close)	%	20	

Continued

		Examples	Your numbers
=			
Step 4: No. of interested prospects needed to meet monthly goal (no. of sales units / conversion rate)		100/0.20 = 500	
=			
Your team's activity conversion rate (from 1st contact to interested prospect)	%	10	
Step 5: Amount of activity per month to generate interested prospects (no. of interested prospects / activity conversion rate)		500/0.10 = 5,000	

Now that you have done the math, ask yourself these questions:

- Are the 'interested prospects' numbers (Step 4) I expect my team to meet every month/week/day realistic with the time and resources available to them?

- Is this level of activity or number of leads (Step 5) the sales team is expected to generate monthly/ weekly/daily realistic/doable for the team I have?

If the answer to any of these questions is "no," then you can probably see why the team thinks the targets are unrealistic.

In *Can Your Sales Team Actually Achieve Their Stretch Goals?* authors Zoltners, Sinha and Lorimer also recommend the following to help you see if your goals are realistic.[2]

- **Look for goal padding.** Check whether and how much goals have been inflated or padded as they've been passed to the sales team compared to what was originally discussed.

- **Set a benchmark for the percentage of your sales team that must accomplish their goals.** For instance, if your mark is at 60–70% and the percentage of salespeople on the team that make their goals is close to your benchmark, then it is probably realistic. But if the vast majority is failing then take a look at your goals.

- **Not everyone on your sales team is going to be a high performer.** If your high performers seem to be leaving and the overall goal attainment of the sales team is low, your sales goals may well be unrealistic.

If, after the exercise, you answered, "No, my goals are probably not realistic," ask yourself these follow-on questions:

- Are we inflating or padding the goals that were originally decided?

---

2   Zoltners, A, Sinha, PK and Lorimer, SE (2016) "Can Your Sales Team Actually Achieve Their Stretch Goals?" Harvard Business Review. https://hbr.org/2016/07/can-your-sales-team-actually-achieve-their-stretch-goals

- What resources do I need to put in place to get to my numbers?

- Do I need additional members on the sales team?

- Do I need more marketing support?

- Are there different strategies my sales team needs to be applying to get better quality leads?

- Does our marketing strategy align to provide the support sales needs?

If your answer is "YES, my goals are realistic," ask these questions:

- Have the market conditions changed in the last six months?

- Are they expected to remain the same or change?

- What major factors could affect these numbers?

- Are your goals in sync with market reality?

You probably have in place some kind of a performance management system that cascades goals down by product lines, between sales teams etc, and is more exact.

The goal of this exercise is simply to take the perspective of how things might appear on the ground and get a clearer understanding of what it might be like to walk in the shoes of your salespeople. With a new perception comes a different understanding and awareness of challenges that may have been overlooked and the ability to work together to solve those challenges.

At the end of the exercise, very different conversations were taking place among the executive team. One executive mentioned, "Based on this, John's team needs ninety appointments a week, which seems high." The focus then shifted to how to get those appointments for John. Marketing shared ideas on an online video campaign they had been discussing to promote the product in the market which would help them reach a wider audience and help create more visibility and appointments for the team.

The goals didn't change. Instead, the ideas that emerged resulted in getting sales teams on the ground more support to get the job done.

Blind spot #2: Higher goals will create higher sales

"We need to challenge our sales team with higher goals. They sell more, they earn more, that's a pretty good incentive to meet their goals," reasoned Sean, the CFO.

Google "high sales goals" and you will come across multiple forums that show conversations among top salespeople about what they consider "high" goals. I came across one sales forum where the conversation thread went something like this:

Tech sales pro: I beat my goals last year, and they reward me by giving me even higher goals. It's really frustrating. What should I do?

Comment 1: The same thing happened with me last year. I worked like crazy and beat my goals, but the expectations never stopped. I think it might be better to quit and find a new company while you're at the top.

Comment 2: Hold off on your goals so that they don't raise it next year.

Contrary to popular belief, having high goals doesn't always motivate your sales team to work harder. This blind spot represents the problem of not knowing how to strike a balance between encouraging for top performance and setting impossible goals.

In fact, the practice of implementing "stretch goals" is often eyed with suspicion because often that has become a way of disguising unrealistic expectations as challenging expectations. Stretch goals have also earned a reputation for goal padding, where goals are inflated as they move down the organization because each level of management tacks on a percentage to the goal to secure themselves against a bad quarter.

Upper-level management may find themselves wondering, "Why don't high sales goals work to motivate salespeople to sell more? After all, their remuneration is directly impacted by achieving them!" The simple answer is that it's not a question of remuneration; it's a question of morale.

When goals are interpreted as unachievable, salespeople will disengage. They become discouraged when they believe the goals presented are beyond reach. When they don't believe in the goal, they might give it a try—despite the inner voice in their heads and pressure from management—but at the first sign of defeat, they'll be ready to throw in the towel. The impact: an erosion of confidence, feelings of dejection, and lowered belief in their own abilities, which only perpetrates the vicious cycle.

Our beliefs shape our behaviors and results. In his book *The Winner Effect: The Neuroscience of Success and Failure*, Ian Robertson explains how success and failure have more impact than genetics and drugs. "Winning affects our biochemistry; it increases the dopamine levels in our brains and changes the chemistry of our brain making us more focused, smarter, more confident, and more aggressive. On the contrary, when we lose, the opposite takes effect where our testosterone levels drop making us fearful over time and avoiding situations that are perceived as risky because we associate it with the history of losing."[3]

Achieving sales goals is as much a mental game as it is a tangible practice. Your salespeople can learn the

---

3   Robertson, IH (2012) *The Winner Effect: The Neuroscience of Success and Failure*. London: Macmillan.

techniques of selling but unless they believe in the goal, they will not be able to sell.

Blind spot #3: Mandating the same goals for everyone on the sales team

At the end of one of my training sessions, I asked one of the new recruits who had joined the high-performing sales team a month earlier about her performance. "I am not doing very well," Mary told me. "I have a goal of five units every month. I sold two this month, but that's not good enough. I need to be at five." I knew the market was tough out there with it being an election year in Kenya, and quite frankly, I thought two sales was pretty good given the timeframe and market situation.

Two months later, Mary was let go because of her inability to meet her goals. Her manager confided in me, "Everyone on the team is meeting their goals except Mary. There is pressure from the top, and I had to let her go." I was disappointed because I had seen potential in Mary and knew she was capable of meeting her goals.

Many sales team managers fail to understand that not all salespeople are created equal. Getting a new team member on board and expecting them to perform at the same level as experienced team members may not be realistic.

Learning a new product and industry, and building confidence in your abilities, takes time. Not only do new reps need a chance to adapt, they also need to be given goals that acknowledge differences in levels of experience. Setting the same goals for new reps as the more experienced reps is setting them up for failure. Moreover, comparing their performance with more experienced reps focuses on what is not working vs. what is working. This fails to build the self-esteem necessary to improve and leads to an overall lack of motivation.

Instead, consider having sliding scales or smaller targets for new team members who may not yet have the confidence and knowledge in the product they are selling or even the industry they might be selling into. As they progress from one level to the next, they begin to build confidence. As they experience success in small increments the winner effect kicks in and tackling bigger goals becomes more doable and achievable.

Blind spot #4: Sales is a numbers game—the more you do, the more you get

> "You've got to be before you can do, and do before you can have."
> — Zig Ziglar[4]

---

4   Wright, N (n.d.) "The Little Book of Quotes: Zig Ziglar." https://nevillewright.com/inspirational-neville-wright/little-book-quotes-zig-ziglar

When I first started out in my consulting business, I was intent on the actions I needed to take to achieve the results I wanted. My peers would tell me, "Sales is a numbers game," and they assured me that I just needed to keep pushing to be successful. That seems pretty logical, my analytical finance brain reasoned, so I stuck to the formula.

I achieved some success, but the consequence was that I was completely burned out. I actually started to see a higher rate of rejections than sales, and it began to take a toll on my confidence and self-esteem. I would push myself harder and apply willpower to get more done, but the results didn't change much, and I felt like a failure.

It wasn't until I understood the principle of "Be, Do, Have," that my results started to change. Let me explain what I mean by that. Consider it in the context of a mathematical formula:

$$Be \times Do = Have$$

- **Have:** the sales targets your team have to achieve.

- **Do:** the activity needed to get results. For example, "Do" would be scheduling the target number of sales meetings needed to close a sale.

- **Be:** belief in your own ability or constant personal development. For instance, for your sales reps to get things done, they have to first believe that they can help the prospect solve their problem or perhaps have confidence in their abilities to talk with senior executives.

If you think of this as a mathematical formula, this means that success comes as a result of both the Be (self-belief) and the Do (getting the activity done). Focusing on one without the other will be a zero.

When the pressure for sales is intense, the directive from above is focused on ramping up activity, getting more business in the pipeline, and doing what it takes to get sales. This seems logical. Here's what a typical sales meeting looks like: "We are down on our targets. We need to bump up the activity levels and get more appointments."

Sales teams may put in the effort needed to ride the wave, but activity alone cannot sustain performance. The performance management strategy for improving sales cannot only be focused on improving one side of the formula, the DO. Salespeople, unlike other professionals, have to deal with rejection every single day. Rejection takes a toll on us because it goes against our core human need for acceptance. Personal development becomes key to building resilience. Without incorporating the BE or the personal development in managing performance, expecting sustainable sales growth is unrealistic.

Let me share an example with you. I was working with a client on improving their sales results. During my coaching sessions with senior sales leaders we introduced a new approach to managing performance in sales teams. They had a huge target to meet for their teams. So far they had been pushing for increased activity but that had not brought about the results they expected. Salespeople were discouraged and frustrated. I knew we had to focus on the BE as much as we did on the DO. We implemented three things in our weekly sales meetings:

First, instead of getting straight down to pipeline activity with each rep, the managers would start their meetings with a celebration round and get everyone to share a success. It could be anything from getting a great contact at a company to closing a sale or simply even being thankful for what was currently going on in their personal lives.

The second thing managers did was ask the question, "What has been our biggest lesson from the sales we closed or didn't close?" The attention shifted to learning vs. a beat-up session on why you didn't close the sale. Third, the managers shared a quick recap of the current performance with targets but instead of simply insisting they ramp up activity, they asked these questions:

- "What is working right now in getting appointments?"

- "What can we do to increase the number of appointments we can get?"

Notice that the questions engage the team in solving problems versus focusing on what is not working. Creating an environment that starts with appreciating your current strengths and then using creative thinking to build on them, enables the team to come up with their own solutions. In the process the team starts to look at problems more objectively because they don't have to put up a defense mechanism to deflect blame. We are tapping into their own ability to solve problems. When they come up with solutions, they also believe that it can be accomplished. When they believe in the solution, they will have the tenacity to try a different approach and be open to learning new skills to overcome the problem. In four weeks, the team had landed three large contracts, made headways into the five major accounts and were within 90% of their target.

Get your team to fire on both cylinders with *Be* and *Do*.

Blind spot #5: Ignoring the impact you have on the emotional climate of your sales team

According to author Steven Chandler of *100 Ways to Motivate Others*,[5] when leaders get anxious about people's poor performance, they download the anxiety onto their people, thinking that they will motivate their teams. Nothing is further from the truth in getting your team to get results.

I remember an instance when I was working as a financial analyst. Our CFO was a great person to work with, but he could also be stern and demanding when he was under pressure. You didn't want to be around him on those days. If you wanted him to sign off on an important decision, it was better on a day when he was in a good mood. We would stop by his PA's desk and ask her, "How is Jim doing today?" before we ventured in. When Jim came to the office on days like this, usually after a board meeting, we knew what the day was going to be like, and it set the tone for everyone around. You could sense the pressure everyone was working under.

Emotions within a team are contagious, and they influence the way we behave. As a leader, you have a strong influence on the emotional climate of your team even when you're not aware of it. The team takes its emotional cues from the leader. Your emotional state

---

5   Chandler, S and Richardson, S (2008) *100 Ways to Motivate Others* (revised edition). Franklin Lakes, NJ: Career Press.

sets the stage for how your team will feel and behave around you and how much of themselves they should put into their work.

What is even more interesting is that when a company goes through crisis mode, people are not sure how they should behave in unfamiliar situations and they look to the leader for guidance.

During the 2009 financial crisis in the USA, banks were under a lot of pressure to deal with bad loans. it was an uncertain environment to say the very least. With so many banks going under or merging, no one was sure where they were headed. I was working with the relationship managers at the bank. I knew they were under immense pressure to get new accounts. At that time, Dana was the sales director for the team. Dana was one of those people who could still keep a level head and stay positive despite what was going on around her. She understood how the uncertainty was affecting her team. At their weekly meetings and in between she made it a point to keep the team posted on what was happening in the market, the effect, if any, it would have on their team and how they would work through the situation.

By addressing things head on she built trust and gained influence within her team who would otherwise have relied on the grapevine. As a result, her department stayed on task with the numbers and had no lay-offs. When the leader is not expressive an emotional power vacuum develops and a team member who is the most emotionally expressive can become more influential regardless of their status on paper. The more emotionally expressive you are as a leader the more influence you have on the people around you.

If you have high expectations and demand results, focus on creating a positive emotional climate for your team. Research on emotional intelligence shows that positive emotional states such as joy, interest, contentment, and pride, can increase performance by 25–30%.

In his article "Emotional Capital: The future balance sheet asset," author Marty Newman, the leading expert on emotional capital, shares the following research by the Gallup organization in their report *The State of the Global Workplace*: "Data from 47,000 employees in 120 countries around the world shows a powerful relationship between the levels of emotional well-being, employee engagement, and profitability." Even companies that reported at least a basic level of engagement outperformed their competitors by 19% on average.[6]

When people feel safe or experience positive emotional states, the part of our brain called the prefrontal cortex that is responsible for complex thinking and planning, is activated. We're able to absorb new

---

6   Newman, M (2015) "Emotional Capital: the future balance sheet asset." https://martynnewman.com/emotional-capital-the-future-balance-sheet-asset-you-wont-ignore

information faster, think more strategically and creatively, and reach decisions more quickly.

Chapter summary

1. When we think of sales growth, the tendency is to look outward. Often, the reasons for poor growth lie internally and get overlooked because familiarity with the status quo can blindside us. It takes a conscious effort to tackle the internal factors for sales growth.

2. The perspective dilemma: Take the goal to activity conversion exercise to find out if your goals are realistic.

3. Contrary to popular belief, having high goals doesn't always motivate your sales team to work harder. When goals are interpreted as unachievable, salespeople will disengage and get discouraged because they believe it's out of their reach. The impact: an erosion of confidence, dejection, and a lower self-belief which only perpetuates the vicious cycle.

4. Not all salespeople are created equal. Setting the same goals for new reps as the older reps is setting them up for failure. Moreover, comparing their performance with older reps focuses their attention on what is not working vs. what is working, and doesn't build self-esteem.

5. Achieving sales goals is as much an inside game as it is an outside game. Understand and apply the principle of "Be, Do, Have" to sales.

6. Emotions within a team are contagious and they influence the way we behave. As a leader you have a strong influence on the emotional climate of your team even when you're not aware of it.

3
Align Your Boardroom With Your Front Line

Jim is the CEO of an insurance company that is rapidly expanding across Africa. One day, we were talking about some products they had launched recently that were not performing to their expectations. "I believe we have a very sound strategy in place for launching this," said Jim. "As an executive team we have devoted time and effort defining our strategy that I believe will set us apart from our competition. We've looked at market trends and this product can help us grow our market share. I know that the executive team is aligned with the strategy, but we can certainly do a better job at getting the middle management and frontline sales teams involved in the execution. I am still not seeing that in the numbers for this product. That's where I feel like we're missing the boat."

Different perspectives

There are always two sides to a coin. In separate interviews with the sales directors and managers responsible for integrating the product into their existing portfolio and getting their sales teams on board to sell, here is what I heard.

The sales director's perspective

"At the end of the day we are responsible for achieving the overall sales targets for our department. This product is just one part of our portfolio and one that requires me to get my team to focus on a completely different target market. At the end of the day they only have so much time. Moreover, the commissions from this product are much less than the commissions they earn from promoting our primary line.

While there is a mandate from above for the need to grow the sales for this line, and we encourage them, the bottom line is that for the time and effort they need to put in, it's probably not worth their while. That's why we're not hitting our numbers. We shared these concerns when we were launching this product but I am not sure that was really heard. I believe the only way to fix this is to get a separate team focused on just selling this product."

The sales team's perspective

"I am under pressure to meet my goals. We have told our managers that we need more support from marketing to help us penetrate a new market. Right now, we don't have that and it falls squarely on us to market it and sell it. This will take time and effort and quite honestly, I can't afford to get behind on my sale goals. My manager is not going to be happy if I don't bring in the numbers."

Translate strategy into action

Like most CEOs, Jim and his team placed a high priority and focus on formulating a business strategy that enabled them to stay ahead of their competition and take advantage of the opportunities the market presented. While this is important and hard work, it doesn't end here. Leadership is about maximizing your impact through your teams and how well the business strategy gets implemented by each person in the organization. I think the following quote says it all:

> "Success doesn't necessarily come from breakthrough innovation but from flawless execution. A great strategy alone won't win a game or a

battle; the win comes from basic blocking and tackling."
— Naveen Jain, entrepreneur[7]

If you have been working on and discussing strategy for the last couple of months with your peers, it is easy to forget that the mid-level management and front-line team have not been involved in those conversations and don't have the benefit of the knowledge you have. They are probably hearing your strategy for the first time.

Recognize that the sales team is not going to adapt immediately, unless they have more clarity around the strategy and comprehend their role in the execution of it. A great question to break though the bias is to ask, "What are our managers saying, and why does it matter?"

Conducting the "how" test

In their article "Can You Say What Your Strategy Is?"[8] authors David Collis and Michael G Rukstad offer an interesting insight. If you can't summarize your strategy in thirty-five words or less, it's not as clear as you think it is and, chances are, each person who hears it has their own version.

---

7   BrainyQuote (n.d.) "Naveen Jain Quotes." www.brainyquote.com/quotes/naveen_jain_416008
8   Collis, D and Rukstad, MG (2008) "Can You Say What Your Strategy Is?" https://hbr.org/2008/04/can-you-say-what-your-strategy-is

In the opinion of Collins and Rukstad, having a goal is not nearly as important to overall clarity as having a strategy that defines the goal it is meant to achieve. It is also more powerful because your teams can internalize it and use it as a guiding light.

Your strategy defines "what we will do to achieve the goal," and probably also outlines "how we will do it" on a high level. Since your managers are responsible for driving change on the front lines, it is critical that middle managers have total clarity on how to implement their action plans, measurement criteria, and success indicators so that they can drive change at the front lines.

Two questions that are often unanswered for your middle management and employees—questions that profoundly impact execution—are:

1. "How does it relate to my role?"

2. "How will it achieve expected results?"

Pushing for implementation without addressing these two questions prevents the execution of your strategy and often results in scenarios such as Jim's.

Answering the "why" questions

I was invited to sit in on a sales meeting by the sales director of Jim's company, and it went something like this. "Our strategy is to become market leaders with our ABC product to the healthcare sector. We have aggressive goals we must meet which you probably saw. I believe we can do this." The director then went on explain the new targets, the types of clients to approach and gave more details on the "how".

I noticed that the meeting focused primarily on the "what" and "how". The "what" and the "how" deal with logic while the "why" deals with emotion. People are driven by their emotions and if we neglect this important fact it's hard to get buy-in for your strategy and also harder for the team to be motivated and bring in their best work.

Author Simon Sinek says it best in his Ted Talk and book *Start with Why*, about how leaders can inspire co-operation, trust, and change. To quote Sinek, "When a WHY is clear, those who share that belief will be drawn to it and maybe want to take part in bringing it to life."[9]

If you want engagement, get good at starting with the "why" before you get to the "what" and "how".

Addressing the "what-ifs"

There will be situations that challenge your current assumptions and strategy. You have probably

---

9   Sinek, S (2011) *Start with Why: How Great Leaders Inspire Everyone to Take Action*. London: Penguin.

considered these when designing your strategy. An important aspect that sometimes gets left out is looking at what could go wrong with your strategy from the perspective of the people executing it.

Planning for success also means planning for what could go wrong. Greg Githens of Leading Strategic Initiatives suggests proactively asking the following three questions to minimize mistakes that might happen and if they do, how to deal with these situations instead of coming to a grinding halt:

1. What are the mistakes that I must not make?

2. What are the mistakes that others must not make?

3. What resources do I have to deal with the unexpected?

According to Githens,

"The first two questions recognize that people make mistakes, and it is the response to mistakes that causes trouble. The important part for us as leaders is to understand that our reaction and response to a situation sets the tone for how effectively a situation can be resolved."[10]

---

10   Githens, G (2011) "Interpreting Vague Strategy: The Compact Approach." https://leadingstrategicinitiatives.com/2011/08/30/interpreting-vauge-strategy-the-compact-approach

Inspire your front line to execute on your strategy

When I work directly with teams, my first question is, "What is your understanding of your sales strategy?" Often, the answer is vague and something like, "We should be selling more of this product to this market." Rarely can someone tell me what that means for them and their individual plan for implementing the strategy. They've been given a target but don't know the "why" that affects their ability to sell the product.

This was the case with one of my real estate developer clients. The team had blown their targets through the roof for one product but were behind on their targets for the other product. I know for a fact that the reason for low sales for product two was not their ability to sell or lack of knowledge. In my conversations with them, I found that they didn't quite understand why they were being pushed to sell the second product when clearly the first product delivered on the promise to the customer and was of a higher value. Given that they didn't buy into the product themselves, it was no wonder that sales of the second product were low.

It's easy to fall into a rhythm of getting things done without taking time to engage with the team. While the simple reasoning, "We have to meet numbers, so sell this product and let's get it done," sounds efficient, it actually leads to longer sales cycles and a high percentage of salespeople not meeting their quotas. The most important element that will drive growth in your company is taking time to connect with your team and explain the "why".

Make your strategy relatable before attempting to implement it

This exercise works great in translating and communicating strategy, and when one of our clients adopted it they saw each department gain clarity around their specific roles. The first step involves getting the heads of departments together to review the strategy in the context of the following questions:

- Why are these objectives important for my department?

- What do they mean for us?

- What results do we need from my department to meet our strategy objectives?

- How does the strategy relate to the way we work in my department?

- What do we currently do that helps us achieve it?

- What do we do that stops us from achieving it?

- How can we ensure that we work toward it?

- What external factors stop us from achieving it and what can we do about them?

- How can we build greater engagement within the team?

Going through this exercise helps the heads of departments look at their business strategy in the context of everyday activities and enables them to visualize the activities needed to implement it. As they go through the process, not only does the strategy begin to crystallize into specific actions for their department but it is also instrumental in helping them own and internalize it.

Next, they go through the same steps with their team. The process helps gets buy-in because their team members are forced to think strategically and relate to the bigger picture. When they can see how their roles help accomplish the strategy and get an understanding of why things are done in a certain way, they no longer feel like cogs in the wheel.

This approach also opens the door for brainstorming solutions to blocks that might appear along the way. When employees are involved in figuring out how to resolve issues and problem solve, there is more engagement. It also helps them see how everyone's work and roles are driven by the same strategy and how they all connect in the big picture.

Embed strategy into daily routine

The 90-day implemetation plan

Once team members are clear on how strategy relates to their roles, the leaders focus on implementation plans. This is where the rubber meets the road and the work of implementation begins. Sales teams spend half a day breaking down their goals into daily activity levels and, more importantly, focus on their own strategies for lead generation and sales conversion to hit their targets.

During such meetings managers work one-on-one with sales reps to refine their action plans and get into tactics. For instance, one of the sales reps had referrals as a strategy. Both he and his manager worked to identify his best referral givers and then upgrade the second tier of clients on his database to become active referral givers.

Does this take time? Of course. It's like the saying goes, one hour of planning can save eight hours of fruitless activity. By taking time to anticipate obstacles, think through solutions, and prepare a plan for action, daily activities have more focus and purpose. It also prevents sales reps from heading off on a tangent.

The frequency of revisiting your plan once a quarter keeps the strategy alive and kicking. It also keeps the momentum going and allows people to brainstorm, think creatively and share ideas.[11] Moreover, if you are comparing your actual results and plans against your strategy every quarter, there is time to adjust your

---

11   Edinger, S (2012) "Three Cs of Implementing Strategy." https://
     forbes.com/sites/scottedinger/2012/08/07/three-cs-of-
     implementing-strategy/#13e73dcc5fb1

plans instead of waiting till the end of the year to figure out if your strategy worked.

Show your team the ROI

While most salespeople have already calculated their commissions with new targets, take it a step further to emphasize the return on investment for each member and discuss the possibilities that open to them when they accomplish their goal.

One of my clients has taken to setting a personal goal and a celebration goal that is tied to them achieving their sales goal.

Keep the strategy alive and kicking

As your sales team implements their plans, have your sales managers refer to the strategy as a guiding light during team meetings, coaching sessions with team members, and when reviewing sales situations and interactions with clients. A great question they can ask during team meetings is, "How is this helping us achieve our strategy?"

The more you ask, the more it sticks and soon you might find your sales team and sales managers using that question as a reference point in implementation.

Keep an eye on market trends and make it part of your culture

Make it part of the job description of your sales managers and sales directors to proactively translate information they get from their sales reps about customers into trends that might be happening in the marketplace. It is easy for sales managers and directors to get caught up in day-to-day implementation and meeting targets to the point that they lose sight of how the market might be shifting. Not only does this keep your strategy relevant but keeping an eye on the horizon helps you catch the wave faster and stay ahead of the competition.

Here is what Sally, a director of sales, has initiated within her team. By asking these questions she has created a culture where each one of the team members is consciously paying attention to what they hear out there:

- Why did customers buy from us?

- Why did we lose the sale?

- What are customers moving toward and why?

- What types of customers are we attracting?

- What are our customers asking for that we should be investing in?

- Where do you see an opportunity for growth?

Sally also gives special recognition to those who share valuable insights during team meetings. Once every two months Sally makes it a point to meet with key customers for the sake of simply understanding what is going on in the marketplace and asks the above questions to gain insights. She also subscribes to resources offering the latest market news.

Share market insights

Monthly meetings are not just for reporting. Besides the regular reporting, make "reporting market insights" an agenda item.

At Sally's company, during monthly reporting meetings to the senior management, sharing insights on the market is an important point of discussion. It starts the conversation between marketing, sales, and operations to translate how external factors have a bearing on business operations. For instance, after one such meeting, marketing was able to share information from their research on how new legislation for one of their target industries could create an opportunity for a line of their solar products. While sales had heard discussions around that, it was a great way to confirm their findings and actively start looking at companies that would have a need for their products once the legislation went into effect in the next six months.

This became an important opportunity for Sally as she shared the information with her reps and assigned companies that would be affected the most. By proactively assigning reps to these companies and working with marketing to clarify the messaging, Sally's company was better positioned to reap sales when the legislation kicked in and had the first-mover advantage.

I am convinced that had it not been an initiative by the CEO to make strategy a "living thing" in the company and create a culture to cascade strategy down to the frontlines, these opportunities would have been missed.

Chapter summary

1. Take into account the multiple and unique perspectives in the organization so you can understand what each person is saying and why it matters.

2. To get engagement you must start with "why" before you move on to the "what" and "how." Unless your team understands why the strategy is important, they won't be willing or able to implement it.

3. Pushing for implementation without addressing the two "how" questions for your middle management and sales reps prevents the execution of your strategy.

4. Make your strategy relatable before attempting to implement it by reviewing the strategy in the context of the strategy questions.

5. The frequency of revisiting your plan once a quarter keeps the strategy alive and kicking. It also keeps the momentum going and allows people to brainstorm, think creatively, share ideas, and adjust course.

4

Your Sales Process Impacts Your Team's Ability To Close New Business

A mber, the country director of a risk management company, and I met to talk about her sales team. She shared the following.

"We have a fairly decent process where we have defined the steps we need to take in order to take an interested prospect all the way through to signing the contract for our security system. Our reps know what information to share with business owners and homeowners, and they more or less follow the process. But this is where it gets a little tricky. Our reps send our prospects the information they need and book a meeting, but then they have trouble closing. They lose control of the process, find themselves chasing after prospects forever, and end up in the follow-up loop. Part of the challenge we have is finding out how many of these prospects are real prospects and the value of business we have on hand. We will have prospects that buy from us but others that don't. It's really hard to say what we'll be closing at the end of the month. Most often, we're not sure why they didn't buy or where the deal fell through."

Sometimes, it's easy to pin the problem on the abilities of your salespeople and overlook the fact that the real problem may actually be buried in your sales process. This chapter looks at the sales process in a little more detail. These insights will be valuable to your sales leaders when it comes to implementing ideas on managing pipelines and team performance. I feel that by giving you a peek into how sales conversions happen, you may also spot opportunities to improve overall buyer experience, drive collaboration among different departments and eliminate recurring problems.

What exactly is the sales process?

If the word "process" makes you wince and think of your last dental appointment, don't go there. It's not as complicated or painful as that. But what exactly is the sales process?

It is the steps and actions that your sales teams take with a prospect to convert them to a customer.

Broadly, the steps in your sales process probably look like this:

- Look for new prospects
- Connect with them via phone, email, or a meeting to gather more information or determine if they are a viable prospect
- Research their company's needs
- Present your product or solution to them in a presentation
- Achieve a buy-in commitment from all decision makers
- Negotiate
- Get a signed agreement or contract
- Close the sale

You've probably defined the steps that need to take place to get a prospect from being interested to actually booking a sale. Your team probably also has the knowledge and tools to move prospects to the next step in your process, get them to sign the agreement, and hand them over to customer services/operations to take over.

The part that may get a bit fuzzy, however, is this:

- How long are prospects taking at each stage?
- How many prospects fall off the train?
- What are the reasons they don't buy?

If you're wondering, "Do I have this process in place?" or, "How is this a problem?" you are asking the right questions. Let's do a quick test.

How to find out if your sales process is working for you

The Sales Process Questionnaire

Questions to ask yourself	Yes/No
1. Does your team ever tell you that they've given all the information to the prospect but then somehow the prospect goes "silent" and they lose control of the process? While some customers end up buying, others don't, and it's difficult to say why.	
2. Is it a struggle to figure out how much business there is in the pipeline (and what it's worth)?	
3. While your sales team generally follows the same steps to bring on a new customer, is there consistently a huge variation in the amount of time it takes to close a customer?	
4. Do you have a reliable forecast of the business in your pipeline?	
5. Are you able to measure the number of prospects you have at each stage in your process?	
6. Do you have an idea of how long prospects should stay at each stage in the process? (This is important for you to know, especially if your sales team tells you at every meeting that they are waiting on the prospect to get back to them.)	

Continued

Questions to ask yourself	Yes/No
7. Are you able to see the total revenue that is sitting in your pipeline and know with a fair degree of certainty what the numbers will look like when they come out at the other end?	
8. Have you clearly defined what information the prospect needs to move forward at each stage in the process?	
9. Does your sales process become the source of information for designing your next marketing campaign in terms of targeting leads? (If you're thinking, "We've never really talked about this," then it's a great opportunity to consider.)	

If you answered "Yes" to 1–3: Chances are, your sales process is not being managed for results, or it may not be in line with how buyers want to purchase from your business.

If you answered "No" to 4–9: Your sales process may be unclear and largely left to chance, which is affecting your sales team's conversion rates.

What an effective sales process can do for you

If you find yourself asking, "Is it worth it to stop and look at our sales process when we should be focusing on the goals for the quarter?" To answer your question, absolutely.

Nine times out of ten, I find sales reps focusing mainly on increasing the number of leads as a primary strategy to get to their sales target. While this is great, the sooner they get better at converting the leads they have, the faster they get to their goals.

Do the math!

Your sales revenue is equal to your number of leads multiplied by your closing rate. Your closing rate can be defined as the number of leads your salespeople need to talk to before they will close a sale. (For example, if they have to meet with ten prospects to close two sales, the close rate is 2/10 or 20 percent.)

Consider the following scenario.

Sales rep A = 10 leads worth $1 million × 20%

= $2 million in sales revenue

What if, without adding any new leads, Sale Rep A could improve their closing rate from 20% to 30%? Watch how the numbers change.

Sales rep A = 10 leads worth $1 million × 30%

= $3 million

That equals additional revenue of $1 million per sales rep. In other words, if you had a team of ten reps and their average closing rate, as a team, went up from 20% to 30%, it would equal a $10 million increase in sales for the team overall and $10 million closer to your target.

Optimization is key

This is the value of knowing and optimizing your sales process—to enable your sales team to improve their conversion rate.

Optimizing your sales process is all about identifying where small changes in your process can yield big results, whether that means creating tools, providing information kits to help overcome objections along the way and move the prospect forward, or better focusing your marketing campaigns on the target market. It also helps you set parameters for prospects and salespeople alike. When you have clearly defined how long a prospect needs to stay in a particular stage, the excuse of "I am waiting on a client" goes away.

The eight benefits of an effective sales process

Benefit #1: Create clarity

Your sales process helps you clarify the exact steps your prospect takes in the journey to buy.

A customer sales journey might be:

- Step 1: Contact prospect and send information

- Step 2: Set appointment for first meeting

- Step 3: Conduct presentation to purchasing committee

- Step 4: Send proposal

- Step 5: Sign agreement

Once you have clarified the steps, assign a completion percentage to each step so you know how far along a prospect has moved in the process.

A clear sales process gives you an understanding and awareness of where prospects get stuck in your process and fall off.

Benefit #2: Reduce time to convert prospects

Your sales process identifies how long a prospect should stay "stuck" at one stage of the process—and when to move on.

I once had a CEO share the following concern with me: "I think that our team needs to get better at understanding how long and how hard to pursue a prospect and when to move on to the next prospect."

Unless you have set a guideline on how long is normal for each prospect to remain in each stage of your sales cycle, it's difficult to say what is too long or too short and determine what kind of action is needed to move things forward.

When your sales manager looks at weekly pipelines, they should see prospects moving along from one stage to another in the expected time. When a prospect is stuck in a stage too long, and your rep has exhausted all the tools to take them forward, then it might be time for your sales rep to move on.

For your salespeople, time is money literally. The more time they spend on prospects that aren't interested, the less time they have to serve prospects who will become clients.

Benefit #3: Generate more accurate revenue projections so you can course-correct

When you have visibility over the leads and where they are in the process, your ability to accurately project your revenue is increased.

For example, if you have fifty prospects at Step 4 (the proposal stage), there is an 80 % chance that the deals will close. In other words:

50 prospects at Step 4 × 80% = 40 new customers

Of course, this might not always be 100% accurate, but at least your revenue projection is based on real data and not a gut feeling. Not only are you able to take the necessary action to move prospects forward, but you can also course-correct if needed and increase the activity level to get to your monthly targets before the month ends instead of being disappointed by leads that didn't close.

Benefit #4: Help prospects decide faster

You can identify what information you need to give the prospect so they can decide to move forward in the sale.

When you are able to see at what stage prospects fall off, it gives you an understanding of the gaps in the process. With this insight, you can come up with a solution to move the prospect forward, perhaps by creating tools or information kits to help overcome objections.

For instance, with one of my real estate clients, we noticed that most of the investor prospects dropped off after an initial call with the sales rep and didn't make it to the next stage (a meeting with the sales rep). By identifying where they dropped off in the process, we realized that they were skeptical in investing because of the fear of making a bad deal and getting cheated, which was a common occurrence in the marketplace. While they wanted to make an investment, they were unsure of how to get the right information to help them decide if they wanted to move forward.

In response, we created a FAQ sheet on the dos and don'ts of investing in the property market and provided it to the company's prospects. In addition, we included research conducted by independent and credible sources on the state of the property market and what indicators to watch out for when making a real estate decision. The reps made it part of the sales process to send out this document right after the call to the prospects. In a span of one month, the average number of monthly appointments per sales rep went up from 0–1 to 3–4.

Benefit #5: Determine whether the issue is the prospect or the sales rep

Your sales process gives you control over the waiting game—after all, your team can only use the "waiting on the prospect" excuse for so long.

The biggest fallacy in pipeline projection is the number of "wait and see" prospects that inaccurately appear as qualified leads when, in reality, they fell off a long time ago. If the same lead stays stuck at one stage for too long, that's a red flag that needs to be analyzed.

Is it that the prospect was not qualified, or is it the skill of the salesperson that needs to be developed? For instance, when you look at a salesperson's pipeline, you might notice that the prospect often gets stuck at a certain stage and doesn't move on. That may be an indication that your salesperson is not adding value to the conversation.

In these instances, an intervention might help their prospect move forward. For instance, you could have your sales rep tag-team with another rep on the next prospect visit. But unless you have defined your sales process, it is hard to pin down the actual problem and make adjustments to improve your conversion rates.

Benefit #6: Consistency in conversions and revenue

You are able to develop consistency in conversion rates and improve prospect experience.

You will always have reps on a team who are simply better at closing a sale than others. In an interview with top performers, we found that salespeople who consistently follow the sales process have a 30% higher chance of closing a sale than those who don't. Why? Because they don't miss important steps along the way. By following a structured process, they keep the prospect engaged.

When the sales process is undefined (in terms of steps and/or timelines for each stage), it is tempting and exciting to move on too quickly to new leads instead of driving existing conversations forward.

Following through each step of the process builds trust with the prospect and keeps them engaged. Plus, from the customer's perspective, it ensures a consistent experience with the sales team, since they are all following the same process.

Benefit #7: Visibility on your marketing campaigns

With visibility on your marketing campaigns you will know where to adjust, when to get better feedback, and how to implement marketing message improvements.

"We get leads, but half the time, those leads don't go anywhere." This is a common complaint that sales departments have about marketing. How do you know if this is true? A well-defined sales process will tell you if it is the quality of the leads or if those leads are being dropped by the salespeople along the way.

If the leads didn't respond or show any interest in the first contact, it's likely that they weren't qualified, and marketing would benefit from the feedback. Having this insight allows the marketing team to adjust the target market for the campaigns. Not only that, but your process will probably be able to tell you that certain categories of clients take longer than others to close. This becomes great feedback for marketing to either change their message, their offer, or to reach out to a different target market altogether.

Benefit #8: Setting the expectations for follow-through

The sales process forces you to look at your buyer's point of view. It helps answer questions like:

- Why do we need this step in the process?
- Why are our internal processes taking so long to deliver information to sales?

In essence, your sales process is similar to an assembly line. Leads come in through one end and hopefully convert into customers after you've taken them through the steps in your process.

The role of a good sales process cannot be overstated. Not only is it critical in setting expectations for your sales reps, it also helps them stay on course and follow through on leads instead of being distracted by the newest or most exciting lead that ultimately won't go anywhere. It instills the discipline to follow through, which is key to conversion. In addition, from a management point of view, the ability to track how leads are moving through—and being able to estimate revenue—is invaluable.

How to create a process that works

Francis is one of the senior sales team members of a real estate developer in West Africa that I train. During one of the sessions on the sales process, he came up to me and said, "You know, the most frustrating experience for me is when I promise my prospect that the paperwork will take two weeks but it takes four weeks because of our internal processes. It makes me look like I don't know what I am doing. It's embarrassing, and even though I have navigated through tough situations like this with clients, it damages my relationship and trust and impacts my ability to ask for referrals from them. My clients have actually told me that they won't give me referrals because our process takes so long. Our competition is doing it so much faster. Why do we even have these processes, anyway?"

Ouch. That has got to hurt!

When salespeople spend time on damage control, trying to make things right, and saving face, it takes time away from prospecting and, more importantly, the chance to get a warm lead through a referral. That was a dilemma most members of the sales team were facing in this case, and it was time to do something about it. So we stepped back and took a look at the sales process and all the steps that a customer goes through to buy from us.

As we walked through the exercise, it was painfully clear that the internal processes required for approval by operations were delaying the time it took to prepare an offer letter and a sales contract for the prospect. It also became evident why the prospect was frustrated at this point.

The approval stage was a good idea at the start to ensure that internal controls were met, but it ended up lengthening the sales cycle. At the end of the day, the main aim of the sales process is to make the sales cycle efficient and reduce the time it takes for a buyer to commit.

When we identified the red flags, we facilitated a brainstorming session between the sales and operations departments to solve the problem. The approval process was cut down to a twenty-four-hour period from a three-day process and overall cycle time reduced by 22%. Sales reps felt more in control when making promises to their customers while giving operations enough time to handle the internal paperwork.

So how can you create a process that works to improve conversion rates and brings you closer to the sale?

Eight ways to improve your sales process

Way #1: Review your sales process—ask your sales team where the process breaks down and what customers are saying

Facilitate a brainstorming session with all departments that are responsible for providing salespeople the tools to allow them to move the prospects toward the sale.

One of the things I have found useful is to have white-board sessions where we chart out the entire process step by step like we are doing it for the first time. It is amazing that even though everybody on the sales team is familiar with the process, new ideas spring up and bottlenecks are highlighted more quickly. It's as if we are seeing things in a completely new light and working as a team creates more energy. Keep the conversation focused on solving problems and not on blaming either the client or your peers.

As you move from one step of your process to the next, ask these questions:

- What happens at this stage that deters the prospect from moving forward?

- What did we do well at this stage that kept the prospect interested and ready to go to the next stage?

- What can we do to prevent this scenario from happening that causes the prospect to lose interest in us?

- How can we add value/keep them interested in moving forward?

Way #2: Determine whether your process is designed from the perspective of your customer or your company

If you're looking at your sales process from the perspective of your internal process alone, you'll miss seeing how your customers want to experience it.

Most often, our processes begin with an assumption of how we think the customer would like to experience it. A powerful tool for testing your process is to conduct a mystery shopping experience on your products. You'll quickly see where the holes are and where your process breaks down vs. trying to analyze it from the inside out.

The sales process should be determined by your customer's habits and how they want to buy. That means having a thorough understanding of who your ideal customer is and at what points they want to engage with you.

In the book *New Experts*,[12] author Robert Bloom talks about how little control you have as sellers over the process. Gone are the days when companies had the upper hand in dealing with customers and expected them to comply with their process. Modern buyers are savvy, and the sooner you break out of the old mold of feeling that you have an upper hand in the process, the

---

12 Bloom, RH (2010) *The New Experts: Win Today's Newly Empowered Customers at Their 4 Decisive Moments*. Austin, TX: Greenleaf Book Group.

better you'll be able to engage the customer. Buyers know what they want, and your process should be able to engage with them in a way that they want and be built around that.

Way #3: Ensure that each step in your sales process adds value to the client

When we redesigned the sales process with our real estate client, a key factor that kept getting in the way was the mindset of, "We've always done it this way." This is a paradigm that will cause any company to stagnate. In response, we ended up writing this question in block letters on the whiteboard and going back to it any time we got stuck: "Does this step add value to our customer?"

Jeff Bezos, the CEO of Amazon, keeps an empty chair in the boardroom any time important strategy decisions are being made. The empty chair serves to remind them of the presence of their customer and why they are doing what they are doing.

Author Robert Bloom in his book *The New Experts* quotes a comment from Jeff Bezos during an interview with *The New York Times*, in which he said, "We start with our customers, figure out what they want, and figure out how to get it to them."[13]

---

13 Bloom, RH (2010) *The New Experts: Win Today's Newly Empowered Customers at Their 4 Decisive Moments.* Austin, TX: Greenleaf Book Group.

If you're experiencing a long sales cycle, it's most likely the result of unnecessary steps in your process that have become a blind spot. Ask these questions:

- Do we really need this step in the process?

- How does this add value to the client?

- Does this step make it harder for the customer to do business with us? And if so, how can we make this easier on our customer?

Way #4: Add value at each step of the process

This task is all about making your sales process work in terms of improving your conversion rate. Once you have identified the gaps in your process, determined where and why prospects fall off, and have started seeing things from their perspective, you will have an idea of the tools you need to create to counter their objections as they move forward with you. Here are some questions to get ideas on tools to create that can solve their problems:

- What objection does the client have to moving forward in the buying process?

- What tools/information can we provide that will help them see the value they will receive and get them to continue with the buying process?

The real estate developer I mentioned earlier serves as a perfect example here.

Objection: The client had to take a trip out of town to visit the proposed site.

Tools created:

- A virtual tour of the property
- A reservation tool to book and hold his plot for a fully refundable deposit until he had a time to visit the site
- Information kit with copies of the "main title deed"
- Return on Investment sheet—this was created to show the prospect the expected rental income and statistics around capital appreciation

The tools you create to add value will depend on how well you know the customer, their fears, and what it would take to get them to move forward.

Way #5: Keep the client engaged between steps

Understand how your customers buy and what their biggest fears are. In addition, know what you can do to keep the interest alive between the various steps in each stage of the process. Creating value-adding tools is one way.

For instance, with one of my clients in the employee benefits business, they have two major steps during the purchase decision where they must get engagement from the prospect in order for the sale to continue to move forward. The first is meeting with the Human Resources Manager, followed by a meeting with the entire procurement committee. Between those two meetings, they keep prospects engaged along the way by sharing case studies of how reward programs have added to employee engagement with the Human Resources Manager. They also share an ROI tool that allows her to calculate the cost savings from their current program while delivering a much higher quality service.

Way #6: Determine whether prospects are maintaining forward momentum

Is a potential sale really moving forward, or is it just an empty assurance from your salesperson? This is a question that many managers struggle with on a daily basis.

Let's say that your process involves:

1. An initial meeting with your prospect to do a needs analysis

2. A presentation

3. A proposal

Often, reps tell me, "We had a great meeting, and I think Jack will come on board." I am sure the rep has a good reason to believe that, but I also know from experience that a lot of these prospects, despite having had great meetings, never move to the next stage.

But if the rep tells me that we booked a meeting with their partner for a presentation next Monday, I know that the action of the client booking a presentation is a sure sign that the sale is moving forward, and it's not just the rep's perspective. When I look at the pipelines and see prospects in different stages of the sales process, I know that they aren't just the rep's assumptions but an action on the part of the client to move to the next stage.

A really good test of your sales process is to ask the question, "What actions, on the part of the customer, need to take place to move the sale forward?" During my training sessions, I always ask reps to book the next step before they leave the client's office, even if that means booking a phone meeting or an email confirmation on something you need. Getting them to confirm the next step will show you whether they are really engaged with you in the process and want to move along.

Way #7: Define how long each step should take

The question of how long each step in the sales process should take is one I get asked often. The answer to that is two-fold.

First, find out how your target customer likes to buy. For instance, when we were redesigning the steps in the sales process of the previously mentioned real estate developer, we realized that we had allocated three days to preparing a letter of offer for the customer. Those three days were there to give us time internally to get the letter ready. However, our best clients, usually savvy investors, were used to seeing the process go much faster and expected it within twenty-four hours. By figuring out how to accelerate the back end of the process, we reduced that to a day, which suited the customer perfectly.

Second, carefully examine the results of prior deals. Take a look at the last ten to twenty deals you closed. How long did the process take from start to finish? Did they take more or less the same time? That's a quick way to determine whether the time you have allocated in your cycle is adequate. Also, take a look at the last five deals that didn't close. How long did they sit in your pipeline? You might notice that the deals that took longer than the timeline you determined for your sales cycle were impacted by factors such as the industry, the size of the company, the decision makers, or where you got the lead. Getting to know your target market a little better might help you come up with ways to shorten your sales cycle.

Way #8: Decide how to use your sales process to project your pipeline

Do you have a good handle on your pipeline? This is a question that always makes sales managers shift uncomfortably in their chairs. How do you know whether you have an overinflated or overly optimistic pipeline?

Define the stages clearly in your sales process so your reps know exactly what that means and where to place prospects. If you can see how leads are moving along, you have an idea what your quarter looks like. In addition, allocate a percentage of completion to each step in the process. Why is that necessary? So that everybody knows with a degree of predictability what the chances are of hitting your sales targets and what needs to be done on a more proactive basis to actually hit your numbers.

Chapter summary

1. Defining a sales process gives you valuable information you can use to improve your sales results. You will have visibility on your success, be able to create accurate sales projections, solve problems quickly and set realistic expectations.

2. Take the exercise to see if your sales process is working for you.

3. A good sales process creates an efficient sales cycle, improves conversion rates, and reduces the closing time.

4. The sales process should be determined by your customer's habits and how they want to buy. That means having a thorough understanding of who your ideal customer is and at what points they want to engage with you.

5. There are eight ways to improve and streamline a sales process. Review your current process and find out where you'd like to focus in order to improve your buyer's experience and reduce the time it takes to complete a sale.

5

Marketers Are From Mars And Salespeople Are From Saturn

"I had a conversation with Nancy, our head of sales, and I sense a lot of frustration on her part," shared Sylvia, head of HR of an international real estate company based in South Africa. "I know marketing is given a big budget, but I don't know how that translates into real leads for sales. It is creating a lot of mistrust between the two departments. Nancy feels like the marketing campaigns we are running are not relevant to the market. While we have local marketing teams in each country to support sales, they really need to work better together and stop operating as silos."

This sort of thinking is quite common. Regardless of your industry or company, you have probably heard comments such as the following from your salespeople:

- We can't meet our target numbers because marketing isn't sending enough leads.

- Even when they send us leads, those leads aren't qualified and we end up wasting time running after prospects that have no interest in our products/services.

- Our ads and marketing materials don't speak to our customers. They really aren't much help in generating leads—or closing them, for that matter.

- I am not sure that all the social media strategies they're spending their time on really work.

If you've sat through some marketing meetings, you have also probably seen the flip side of it with comments such as these:

- We've generated so many leads from our campaigns! I don't know why sales can't close them.

- I don't think sales actually follows up on the leads we send them. Otherwise, they would have better numbers.

- Sometimes, I think the sales guys don't really know enough about the product.

If the thought has ever crossed your mind that marketing and sales might as well as be from two different planets, you are not alone. A debilitating lack of alignment between the two departments is the reality for most companies.

Seven strategies to get them on the same planet

In the book *Sales Growth*,[14] authors Baumgartner, Hatami and Valdivieso share this case study: "In a global survey of 1,000 marketing and sales executives less than 50% said that they were satisfied with the support sales receives from marketing. Marketers have a higher opinion of the value they provide their counterparts in sales." In other words, most executives agreed that marketers did a great job at competitive analysis and customer insights but were less effective when it came to helping with lead generation.

It takes two to tango and neither marketing nor sales can go at it alone.

They go on to say that companies that do well both at marketing and sales grow faster than those that are only good at either sales or marketing. According to the authors' research, "61% of companies that have

---

14 Baumgartner, T, Hatami, H and Valdivieso, M (2016) *Sales Growth: Five Proven Strategies from the World's Sales Leaders.* Hoboken, NJ: John Wiley & Sons.

both functions working in collaboration have above market revenue growth and also experience higher profitability."

This quote by Jill Rowlsey sums it best. "The new reality is that sales and marketing are continuously and increasingly integrated. Marketing needs to know more about sales, sales needs to know more about marketing, and we all need to know more about our customers."[15]

So how do you ensure that the two align in their results for revenue growth for the company?

Strategy #1: Define your message as a senior leader—overcoming perceptions of bias

In your opinion as a senior leader, which department is more important when it comes to revenue growth? My guess is that you answered, "Both!" Great.

So, where do you invest more resources? And which of the two departments has more influence in getting their objectives met?

The point is that your mindset and actions toward the two departments determines the power position/play

---

15 Callahan, S (2017) "101 Sales and Marketing Quotes to Read Before Setting Your Strategy." https://business.linkedin.com/marketing-solutions/blog/content-marketing-thought-leaders/2017/101-sales-and-marketing-quotes-to-read-before-setting-your-strat

between the two. When the sales department is given more importance because it brings in revenue, recognition for marketing efforts in lead generation and brand awareness can be overlooked and may cause resentment from your marketers. After all, if sales don't have qualified leads, there won't be any sales.

On the other hand, sales can become resentful when marketing is painted as the creative and savvy department that gets resources assigned in the name of brand awareness and all things cool, but campaigns rarely translate into leads.

Clarity around expectations and deliverables is a key element of creating alignment and overcoming the perception of bias. Based on your business strategy and sales targets, you have probably figured out how many leads you need per month or per quarter to achieve your targets. This becomes the basis for establishing lead-generation goals for both marketing and sales. When both departments have clear goals around expected results in terms of lead generation, it sets the tone for collaboration vs. competition.

One way to create objectivity is to separate the marketing budget into branding activities, public relations and communication (if that falls under the umbrella), and marketing campaigns for lead generation. When you have clearly defined KPIs from marketing campaigns, marketing cannot hide behind the "shroud of branding" and will be more accountable for campaign outcomes. Sales on the other hand will have little reason to begrudge the marketing budget when they can see the success of marketing campaigns.

Emphasize the need for collaboration between sales and marketing heads. One of my clients found a really great way to get sales and marketing to collaborate. Besides presenting reports on their individual departments, each head of department is required to report on the effectiveness of collaboration between the departments in terms of specific projects that they are working on, progress, tangible results and measurement criteria. Since it is a collaborative project, there is little room for politics in terms of "showcasing who did more work" as the success of the project is measured along with the effectiveness of collaboration.

Strategy #2: Joint implementation of marketing and sales strategies

While business strategy is determined as a team and both sales and marketing departments have their own initiatives with an understanding of how their roles intersect, when it comes to implementation at the front lines the understanding of how each department's initiatives impact the other gets blurry. Individual departments get so focused on delivering on their KPIs that sometimes it is easy to lose sight of how activities affect the other departments or how they are adding value to their activities.

This tunnel vision leads to scenarios like this one. I had the head of sales of an insurance company once tell me, "Marketing releases all these offers as part of their campaigns and sometimes our sales teams are not even aware of how they work when they are launched. We find ourselves in an awkward position when our customers refer to the offer they've seen in ads and we had no clue it was going to be out so soon."

How do you avoid scenarios like this one?

a) Combined planning

Here is an approach that the head of marketing and sales at a US bank I work with took to create more alignment and synergy. At the beginning of every quarter, they schedule an implementation meeting and invite key members from each department to re-view goals and KPIs for the quarter. The focus of the meeting is to create an "implementation plan" with roles and responsibilities for each department and most importantly, timelines for each department. For instance, at the end of the session, marketing produces a timeline of the campaigns for the quarter and shares it with sales so they can leverage the offers marketing is promoting to their customers.

In addition, sales agree on a timeline and method for providing feedback and insights from clients in response to campaigns. Regular communication is built into the plan and scheduled instead of leaving it up to the teams to communicate. Shared metrics are on the dashboard for these meetings so it keeps everyone focused on the big picture and maintains momentum for results. Clear guidelines on defining a "qualified lead" are agreed upon. This planning process eliminates misconceptions around the goal of the campaigns and creates a shared understanding of the "why" behind them with a platform for inclusion.

b) Clarity around target markets

Another area that the bank in question emphasizes is having marketing and sales work closely together to define their target markets and also specific segments within the target markets. For instance, not only have they found that healthcare is a great target market for them but within the healthcare market, private pharmacies tend to be their best clients. Their lead-generation strategy is laser focused by segment so that both sales and marketing are leveraging their resources to get to their ideal customer profile. During these "target market meetings," they strive to proactively answer the following questions:

- What does my ideal client look like (size, demographics, area, interests, etc)?

- Where do they hang out (eg health magazines they advertise in, associations, events, etc)?

- What are their biggest challenges?

- What can we offer them?

- Why should they be doing business with us instead of our competitor?

- How should we reach them? (How should we start generating interest?)

For instance, in one of the meetings sales mentioned how they noticed prospects coming from one geographical area that was valuable for marketing to understand for their upcoming billboard campaigns and what areas to target.

This approach has not only increased collaboration between the two departments because of a shared understanding of their prospective client but also made their lead-generation efforts smarter. In addition, working together has enabled them to reach their clients in multiple ways. For instance, while marketing is advertising at the pharmacy associations, the sales team is also leveraging the industry networking events to get leads.

Strategy #3: Creating a formal channel for sharing insights and feedback

This is by far the most important part of getting the implementation plan to work. Your salespeople are at the front line with customers and have a pretty good understanding of what is received well and what isn't.

Your marketing department needs that perspective to refine their message.

Often what gets in the way is the lack of a process to make it easy for both sides to share the information. Here are a few ideas that have worked with clients to levarge market intelligence and drive better results.

Regularly scheduled "forward focus" meetings

Here, the primary goal is for marketing to share any new information on promotions, get feedback on their marketing messages or call to action, and share time-lines. Sales has the opportunity to ask questions on how to approach new prospects with offers and leverage the work that marketing is doing to get new clients.

Problem-solving

This platform also makes it possible to solve hurdles quickly. For instance, at one of these meetings, internal process issues were resolved quickly when sales brought up the time lag in transferring leads from marketing. Another issue that got solved quickly was the follow-up email sequence sales could use to get back with interested prospects. The frequency of these meetings also allowed marketing to assess the success of the leads generated against the "qualified lead criteria" both departments had agreed upon and make changes as necessary to improve the quality of leads generated.

Don't forget the customer

During one sales and marketing alignment meeting, we were reviewing the quarterly marketing campaigns. Marketing was really excited about an event they had planned for a promotion. If you looked at it from their perspective you could see why it had made it onto the marketing calendar. One look at the sales team, however, and you could see it written on their faces: "There is no way our prospects are getting out on the weekend to attend this."

What followed next was a great discussion on why the event may not work for prospects and suggestions around how to change it. Interesting ideas were presented, and they had almost agreed to one when I asked the question, "So, if you were the customer, what would you want? And do you care about this?"

What followed was a silence that said, "Probably not."

We went back to the drawing board but with the focus on the customer this time and worked around logistical and internal issues to come up with an event that was a winner.

The point I am trying to make is that it is easy to be blindsided by "the way things are done around here" and accept them unless you consciously stop and ask the question from the perspective of the customer. It's simply a matter of breaking the pattern and the habit of thinking in a certain way. Now, at the start of every sales and marketing planning meetings, we have someone write this question up on the whiteboard as we brainstorm:

"What do I want as a customer, and should I care about this?"

Strategy #4: Consistency in your value propositions

During one of our sessions on value proposition, the sales manager came to me and said, "When I look at the marketing campaigns, I realize we, as the sales team, are not conveying the same message to our customer. Each department is stressing a different element when we should be speaking the same language. We boast about all the companies we have as clients, but our client doesn't really care about that."

Your **value proposition** is your promise of value to your customer of the tangible results they will receive from using your product, service or solution. For example, it states how your product or service solves your customers' problems and delivers the specific results. It also emphasizes why your customer should buy from you and not your competition.

Companies that dismiss the value proposition, in my experience, do great harm to their sales efforts when they take this tool for granted. When your sales reps cannot articulate the specific value that clients derive from using your products or when their message differs from what marketing is promoting, sales conversion rates are impacted. Jill Konrath, author of *SNAP Selling*,[16] talks about creating simple and clear value propositions for your clients that involve these three components:

1. **Business driver**—"primary business reasons that customers would use your offering."

2. **Movement**—or a positive change in something that is important to your client. For example, reduced costs of operations or improvement in employee productivity.

3. **Metrics**—as Jill says, "adding metrics makes your value proposition believable."

Try out this exercise, and you will know what I mean. If you were to ask both marketing and sales departments what their key value proposition is and why customers should buy from you, do you receive a

---

16   Konrath, J (2012) *Snap Selling: Speed Up Sales and Win More Business with Today's Frazzled Customers*. New York: Portfolio.

consistent answer, or are there multiple versions of the value proposition?

Here are a couple of ideas that have worked to create a strong value proposition.

Think from your customer's perspective—create value propositions by target market

One of our client's strategies for the year focused on expanding market share in two major segments. Both marketing and sales had to work together to create a value proposition that would be enticing to the market. Sales shared insights on the client's biggest pain points, and even more importantly, the specific results clients achieved once they used their product. Marketing brought the macro element to the meeting in terms of what was going on in the industry, how new legislation would impact the industry and what it meant for the client. With this information they could craft segment-specific value propositions and pitches that spoke to their client. It included the main business reasons that were important to the client, what kind of change they had experienced as a result of using the product and data to support it.

Both marketing and sales aligned their messages to include the new value propositions. Not only did it create consistency between both departments but ensured that the entire sales team was speaking in the same language to their customers.

Encourage teamwork—have marketing and sales
strategize together

Another client has both marketing and sales teams strategize on the approach they take with large deals they are working on. For instance, a member from each team attends client meetings to better understand the customer's objectives and buying process. Not only does this give marketing an insight into a customer's needs for their next campaigns but enables both teams to prepare a sales presentation that is focused on delivering immense value to their client and focusing the entire value proposition to solve their customer's needs.

Strategy #5: Collaborate on product launch strategies

During a product launch, marketing is usually leading the battle on the front end as operations works on delivery. While sales are usually involved in the process somewhere along the way, they take the back seat until the time comes to sell. Marketing has invested a lot of time and effort in getting the product launch ready and is expecting sales to come on board quickly and start selling once they have taken them through the presentation—only to discover that sales does not share their enthusiasm and brings up reasons why the product will not sell or why marketing it in a certain way will not work to get sales.

If you've been to one of these meetings, you know what I am talking about. The feeling is that of being either unappreciated or frustrated, depending on which side of the fence you might be on. If you want to prevent these scenarios from occurring, have representatives from marketing and sales working together throughout the launch period.

Collaborating frequently will ensure that key information and insights are shared early on which provides ample opportunities for testing and enough time to adjust along the way instead of waiting for feedback at the end and not being able to incorporate it because you are under a time crunch.

Here's an example of what has helped one of our manufacturing clients sell new products successfully. Marketing does a thorough job of researching their target market, conducting customer focus groups to understand what is important to their customer even before they determine their strategy for the launch. While marketing and sales collaborate at all stages of the process, there is a special meeting scheduled between the two departments where the main purpose of sales is to positively challenge the marketing message from the perspective of the customer. At the meeting, sales bring a "client objections list" with them and the insights into why customers will object (based on their experience with current products and meetings with clients). But it doesn't stop there.

Both teams brainstorm on the best way to counter the objections. They make it fun by having the person with the best counter or answer "shoot" the objection. This not only helps marketing refine their message for campaigns but also gives sales the confidence and knowledge to sell the product.

Strategy #6: Create your salesperson toolkit

Leverage your marketing team's immense knowledge in building your sales reps' toolkit. Think beyond the standard marketing materials such as brochures, PowerPoint presentations, business cards, etc. Give your sales reps relevant case studies, market trends, reports, email templates, FAQs checklists, and ROI templates, so they can use these in sales situations.

During a sales training session with a real estate client in South Africa, I was working with the team on how to counter a "market appreciation" price objection. We reached out to the marketing department to see if they had any credible and independent sources of information on market trends and property values that we could use to show our client the potential of property appreciation and rental incomes. The marketing team had the information that was immensely valuable to the sales team, but nobody had thought to reach out and ask. Being able to share this information with prospects gave them confidence in our knowledge and expertise of the market, allowed them to conduct their own due diligence and set us apart as trusted advisors.

Get your marketing department to create valuable content for customers that can be used by the sales team. Don't leave it to the sales team to create that.

Strategy #7: Look out together

It takes all eyes and ears to stay relevant in your target market. Are both departments watching for trends and aware of what is changing in the marketplace, eg legislation and management? And how do they exchange that information with each other?

Make this part of the agenda during regular meetings between departments so it doesn't get missed. Normally, monthly meetings are focused on internal issues and what things need to be changed. It's easy to be caught up in that and to consciously focus on the outside world. One of the items on the agenda for the monthly interdepartmental meetings is "what's going on in the market." While these discussions may be going on at different levels in the organization, by making it part of a formal discussion, the focus shifts to thinking about possibilities and new solutions.

You may realize, after all, that both marketing and sales can speak the same language and be OK with living on one planet.

Chapter summary

1. When both marketing and sales functions in an organization collaborate, sales growth and profitability are higher on average.

2. As a leader, your mindset and actions toward the two departments determines the power position/play between the two. Avoid perception bias by asking yourself these two questions: "Where do I invest more resources? And which of the two departments has more influence in getting their objectives met?"

3. To align your sales strategy, you must align both departments. Which means the senior leaders must get the message right from the start, create clarity of expectations, be objective and emphasize the need for collaboration.

4. Sales and marketing are increasingly interconnected, they must learn to communicate and align their results, and avoid tunnel vision. They can do this through clarity of the target market and combined planning initiatives.

5. Make your value proposition a key tool in your toolkit to improve sales conversion rates. Think from your customer's perspective and be clear on the value you are offering your customer.

6. Determine which of the seven strategies you will use to align sales and marketing for revenue growth for your company.

FACTOR TWO

SAVVY SALES FORCE— RECRUIT THE BEST

6
Bring Out The Best In Your Sales Leaders

W hat is the real role of your sales manager?

I want you to pause and really think about the answer that comes to mind. Perhaps your answer is "to manage a sales team," "to create and implement your sales strategy," "to get results," "to deal with various sales crises and admin stuff," or, rarely said out loud but often true, "to take the pressure off me to meet sales targets." All these answers, in their own way, are right.

The bottom line is that a sales manager achieves your sales targets by leveraging the strengths of each salesperson on their team. Sometimes, though, it is easy to be swayed by a "bright and shiny" résumé and forget the kind of person needed for the role and exactly what role they play in achieving sales targets.

Six incorrect assumptions

Assumption #1: Our top producer will make a good sales manager

"What do you want your new sales manager to be doing?" I asked Linda, the CEO of a hospitality consulting firm in Ghana, as we talked about her plan to fill a newly vacant sales manager position with a certain sales rep she had in mind.

"Well, I would really like to have Judy take on the sales manager role," said Linda. "She is one of our top producers and is well respected by the team. She has a strong client base and consistently brings in new clients. If she could replicate what she does with the rest of the team, that would be fantastic. I need her to start developing the team and training them to do things the way she does. I know she works with them at times. Since she's so good at what she does, I also feel like that intimidates the others a bit. She'll also need to hire the right people, manage them and meet our targets. My only concern is that she has never managed people before, but I think we can train her to do that. I think she can manage the two roles."

Later, my conversation with Judy went something like the following.

"What is your biggest strength in selling, Judy?"

"I think it's the way I network and easily get referrals," she replied. "I love getting out there and making connections that will give me a constant stream of leads."

"You're working with Jane—the new rep—to train her, right?" I said.

"Yes, I am trying to get her to go to networking events with me, but I don't think she really gets the whole networking thing," said Judy. "It's not that she doesn't know what's needed, but I think it is a confidence issue. I would like to spend more time with her, but I have my own goals to meet. Quite honestly, I'd much rather be selling than dealing with people. It's not that I can't manage people, but I find it really draining."

Talk about two completely different perspectives! It is interesting how many companies think that promoting your top salesperson to a manager position is a way of rewarding them and ensuring that their success is replicated by the rest of the team.

The truth: Your best salesperson will not necessarily make the best sales manager.

The two roles of salesperson and sales manager require completely different skill sets. The main role of the manager is to increase sales not through selling directly themselves but by guiding and cultivating the individuals on the team to perform to the highest level they can. In a leadership role, the focus needs to be on achieving results through others to meet targets. Therefore, the strategies that may have been the key to someone's success as a salesperson, such as finding prospects, winning opportunities, and closing, are not directly transferable and will not help you succeed in a role as manager.

Your success depends on how well you can serve your internal stakeholders, ie your team, to meet their targets. It also means finding the right sales reps on your team and maximizing the performance of your existing reps.

Assumption #2: My sales manager will grow into the role and learn how to coach their team and improve performance

According to a study done by the Objective Management Group, "A whopping 82% of sales managers are not effective as sales coaches, which is the most important thing they should be doing with most of their time." In reality, it is estimated that managers spend as little as 10% of their time coaching instead of what should probably be 50%.[17]

When I shared this statistic during one of my strategic retreats in South Africa, one of the country CEOs came up to me and said, "Our sales manager has been talking about how his role needs to focus more on coaching the team than selling, but quite honestly, I didn't give it much credence."

So, if improving performance and coaching the team is so clearly a key role for this position, then in other words, the time that most sales managers devote to this activity certainly doesn't match up. Why are sales managers not spending time coaching?

The truth: Coaching is a learned skill that does not come naturally.

First, it's simply a lack of awareness of the power of coaching to drive results. Most sales managers are inclined to lead in the same way they have seen their own managers lead, which in turn becomes their default management style.

Secondly, coaching is a learned skill that needs to be developed, takes a conscious decision, time and commitment. When there is no culture of coaching

---

17   Gordon, G (2015) "CEOs: What Should You Do About Your Sales Managers?" http://braveheartsales.com/ceos-what-should-you-do-about-your-sales-managers

within the organization to drive performance, it becomes particularly difficult to break out of the pattern and lead differently.

Assumption #3: They'll figure out how to motivate their team

The idea that a salesperson who gets moved up to a sales manager position will somehow magically "figure out" how to motivate their team couldn't be further from the truth. The ability to motivate others is not some latent gene that automatically kicks in just because someone is promoted to a manager's position. Most times, when managers feel the pressure from their bosses regarding results, the default strategy becomes passing the anxiety down to their teams.

The truth: Without a degree of self-awareness and self-leadership, motivating others is just a pipe dream.

As mentioned earlier, in the book *100 Ways to Motivate Others*,[18] author Steve Chandler says, "Often managers lead by passing anxiety down." I thought that was interesting, and as it happened, my next leadership workshop with one of the leading banks in Kenya provided ample validation of that.

During the workshop, managers were asked to do a self-assessment on how they motivate their teams

---

18   Chandler, S and Richardson, S (2008) *100 Ways to Motivate Others* (revised edition). Franklin Lakes, NJ: Career Press.

during tough times. Here is what Geraldine, a senior sales manager, shared with me: "Well, the pressure from above to meet numbers is pretty intense. I know I should really focus on what we can do about the problem but the honest answer is that, at times, I have passed the stress and anxiety down to my team even though that was not the intention. I know it doesn't help anyone, but it happens when you are in an environment like ours."

Then, after a long pause she said, "If we want to motivate our teams to work harder in these situations, we have to work harder on ourselves as managers."

Assumption #4: The sales manager needs to take care of the admin side of sales—after all, that's what their salary is for

Sales managers spend, on average, 40–50% of their time on reports, meetings, managing admin stuff, and sorting out crises. Often the "team developing time" that is sacrificed to deal with admin duties is the part that would actually bring in the sales for the entire team. While somebody must take care of this, is it really the best use of the sales manager's time?

When I ask this question, the response I usually get is, "We don't have enough resources to hire somebody to do that and really, isn't that part of the sales manager's job to stay on top of that stuff?" Fair enough. Let's do the math here for a minute and look at the return on investment for this decision.

Let's say you have a sales target of $2 million per rep and your profitability on sales is about 20%, which means that you have $400k in profit per rep. With a team of ten reps, that adds up to $20 million in revenue or $4 million in profits.

Now, what if your sales manager can help each member on the team improve their numbers by just 5 % by devoting time to problem-solving with them, dealing with their prospect objectives, and helping them win the deal vs. spending that time on support functions. That means you have just added $100k in revenue times ten reps. That equals an additional $1 million in sales and another $200k in profits, which, coincidentally, is probably a minimum of between four and ten times the amount you need to cover the cost of an admin staff member with plenty of change left over.

The truth: People rise to the expectations you set for them.

If the expectation is that the manager will take care of admin stuff, it is natural for your sales manager to cast themselves in that mold. After all, it is easier to spend your time doing admin stuff than coaching and developing people. Solving crises when you really are not required to do so gives you the adrenaline rush of being the hero in the company, but it is short-lived.

Your ability to produce results depends on how much you focus on developing your team vs. moving paper around.

Assumption #5: Hiring new people isn't rocket science

Hiring may not be rocket science, but there's a reason that hundreds of books and studies have been written on how to hire the right people on your team. The hiring process is a learned skill, and it's something you don't want to leave to chance or base on having "a good feeling" about someone.

The truth: Hiring is a learned skill and has a huge impact on hitting sales targets.

Bringing on the right salespeople can mean the difference between hitting or missing your targets. It also means really understanding the type of person you want on your team and being able to strike a balance between the different personality types. I will share more about how to hire the right people on your team when we get to "hiring for results."

Assumption #6. Sales manager should be responsible for selling and managing

Many people believe that sales managers should manage, sell and step in on deals that the reps can't take on. After all, they are still in sales, right? When this is the case, the challenge is often the pressure to meet their own numbers on top of managing and doing admin—which means they aren't as effective in helping others on the team to meet their numbers.

The truth: Above all, sales managers should be there to develop their people.

While the sales manager may need to jump in at times to meet the numbers and take on more of the selling, the primary focus should be on developing the sales team to bring in sales rather than driving sales through their own targets.

Set your sales leader up for success

So, how can you as a CEO support the sales manager and make sure that this position is set up to actually take the burden off your shoulders?

Step #1: Hire correctly

While it's tempting to choose someone who is already doing a great job, don't.

First things first, find out if your sales manager has the required skills needed for the job. The key competencies you need to look for in a sales manager are these:

- Coaching

- Ability to motivate

- Recruiting

- Ability to hold people accountable

- Managing relationships

- Strategic thinking

There are a lots of sales leadership assessments out there that can give you an indication of the leadership ability of your sales managers. One of the assessments I like to use is Profiles XT.[19]

Not only does an assessment make it easy to identify how well someone fits the role, it helps you identify the areas of development for your sales manager.

Step #2: Set the expectations for the role

I recently pulled up this job description for a sales manager on monster.com.

Sales manager responsibilities:

- Sells products by implementing sales plans; supervising sales staff.

---

19 You can check these out at www.profilesinternational.com

Sales manager duties:

- Determines annual unit and gross-profit plans by implementing marketing strategies; analyzing trends and results.

- Establishes sales objectives by forecasting and developing annual sales quotas for regions and territories; projecting expected sales volume and profit for existing and new products.

- Implements national sales programs by developing field sales action plans.

- Maintains sales volume, product mix, and selling price by keeping current with supply and demand, changing trends, economic indicators, and competitors.

- Establishes and adjusts selling prices by monitoring costs, competition, and supply and demand.

- Completes national sales operational requirements by scheduling and assigning employees; following up on work results.

- Maintains national sales staff by recruiting, selecting, orienting, and training employees.

- Maintains national sales staff job results by counseling and disciplining employees; planning, monitoring, and appraising job results.

- Maintains professional and technical knowledge by attending educational workshops; reviewing professional publications; establishing personal networks; participating in professional societies.

- Contributes to team effort by accomplishing related results as needed.

You will notice that the primary role centers on the accomplishment of sales goals through planning and implementing sales strategies. What is interesting is the strong focus on the task-related duties versus team-related roles. When you lay such little emphasis on developing people, it is no wonder people development is put on the back burner. A fleeting mention of people development is probably done in most instances to keep human resources happy.

The irony is that unless you develop your people, the best plans will fail to accomplish your sales objectives. How do you really ensure that sales managers stay focused on their people as well as their tasks?

When Charlotte was hired to take over the sales department of an IT company, she had aggressive targets to meet with her team of fifteen reps. The first thing we did was break down her job into five main categories (coaching, managing pipelines, holding the team accountable, direct selling, and product strategy) that were imperative for achieving results. If you have watched Stephen Covey's video on filling the jar of rocks,[20] you'll know what I mean. We began filling Charlotte's jar with the rocks that would improve team performance first: coaching, managing pipelines, keeping the team on track, selling, and strategy.

We allocated 70% of her time to the first three and 10% to the last two. The remaining 20% was left to accommodate the gravel (eg, crises management, recruiting, compensation plans, etc).

I know you may be shaking your head at this point and saying, "That won't work. We can't even get them to focus on spending 10% of their time on coaching! How are we going to ensure that coaching makes it to the top?" Well, it begins with what you want to achieve. I love the Stephen Covey analogy. If you don't build on the five key areas every day and make them part of somebody's daily job, expect it to be set aside.

Second, we looked at how this would translate into daily activity for Charlotte. How would we ensure that she actually spends at least 50% of her time on developing her team, keeping them on track and coaching them? Well, we set it as an expectation to have one-on-one coaching sessions with the team every week to work through obstacles they were facing. Coaching sessions could be as short as fifteen minutes per employee (that is, 225 minutes a week—about a

---

20 Covey, S (2013) "7 Big Rocks: The productivity system" [video].
    www.youtube.com/watch?v=fmV0gXpXwDU

half a day max). By building coaching into Charlotte's job expectation and ensuring that she set aside time for that, we were able to ensure that the most important part of the job got done.

But in addition to having time built into your calendar, make sure it happens consistently. When it comes to change, consistency trumps intensity every single time.

Step #3: Invest in coaching skills for your manager

Coaching impacts your bottom line positively—it is crucial to your organization's success.

Selling, like sports, is primarily a mental game. I absolutely love the book *The Inner Game of Tennis* by W Timothy Gallwey.[21] As he describes it, "The outer game is played against an external opponent to overcome external obstacles, and to reach an external goal." But the inner game is the one that "takes place in the mind of the player, and it is played against such obstacles as self-doubt and self-condemnation."

---

21 Gallwey, WT (2015) *The Inner Game of Tennis: The Ultimate Guide to the Mental Side of Peak Performance*. London: Pan Books.

To win the game of sales, the focus has to be as much on the inner game as on the outer game. It has been suggested that 50% of successful sales are due to mental skills, with 30% due to technical skills, and the remaining 20% to product knowledge.

Often, organizations will focus on the external game, technical or product knowledge skills when the primary focus should be on helping salespeople find their strengths and figure out for themselves how to best adapt or modify their behavior for success.

Coaching is a critical step to master to succeed in sales in an international market. We look more at coaching and how it can impact your sales success in Factor 4: Sales Coaching—Coach for Performance.

Step #4: Turn failures into learning opportunities—give permission to fail

> "When we give ourselves permission to fail, we, at the same time, give ourselves permission to excel."
> —Eloise Ristad[22]

I remember when I was brand new to selling, right after a sales conversation, my coach Gael would ask me to reflect on the conversation regardless of whether I signed a new client or not. It was an exercise that took only five minutes and many times I did it while

---

22   Walter, E (2013) "30 Powerful Quotes on Failure." www.forbes.com/sites/ekaterinawalter/2013/12/30/30-powerful-quotes-on-failure

driving back to the office. Her two favorite questions were the following:

- What do you think you did well?

- What could you have done differently?

What that allowed me to do was look at the sales situation from an observer's perspective. I would often pick up on things that I would never have thought to change if she hadn't asked me. During one such debriefing, I realized that I had contradicted a prospect without intending to do so, thereby losing the sale. This self-awareness became the catalyst for change and a much more powerful reminder than being told by my manager to "never contradict the prospect."

What Gael rarely did was chastise me for failure. She tapped into my ability to turn every failure into a learning opportunity, thereby shortening my learning curve to get results quickly without damaging my self-esteem and self-confidence.

The value of learning experiences

Managers play a huge role in how they can influence a salesperson's level of self-awareness and learning, which is the prerequisite for long-term change and results. Getting your team to produce results also means recognizing that failures are inevitable and do not automatically mean incompetence. It also means refraining from jumping in and saving them when targets are not met. Creating a culture of performance allows for failure to achieve results; creating a culture of fear keeps everyone safe but rarely gets people to excel.

What is the balance between a risk that is too great and one that will allow for learning and can be corrected quickly? Here's what has worked for one of our insurance company clients in the USA to encourage a culture of risk-taking. At the beginning of every quarter the sales manager and individual team members review their goals for the quarter and create an implementation plan together that details strategies and tactics for achieving the desired results. During the process sales reps have the opportunity to present ideas that would enable them to get the desired results. Not only does this create buy-in but allows sales reps to use their knowledge of the market to test new ideas.

In addition, a very important element of the discussion revolves around what could go wrong and brainstorming solutions to prevent or fix that. Not only does that get the sales rep to think through and refine their ideas but it also gives the manager the ability to foresee potential problems and solve them now versus when it happens. This approach becomes a safety net and allows managers to be more confident in letting their teams test new ideas.

Step #5: Focus your sales meetings on creative problem-solving

An alternative title for this section could be, "How to create a system for motivation." I can't tell you how many times I have heard sales managers tell me, "We need a really good motivational talk to get the team energized and motivated to get results."

First of all, motivation doesn't come from a seminar, it is intrinsic. So if you are thinking of hiring someone to change things around, save the money. Instead, feel free to use some of the ideas we have taken clients through to deliberately create an environment that motivates employees in addition to coaching, creating learning opportunities and joint goal-setting.

While most sales meetings can seem like interrogations into activity and micro-management, it's definitely not the case at the Monday morning sales meeting that Lindsey runs at her bank in South Africa. Her meetings focus on three main things: celebrating successes, brainstorming ways to keep pipelines full, and problem-solving as a group to land new sales opportunities. Lindsey realizes that her team faces enough rejection in the marketplace and takes advantage of the sales meetings to create a positive anchor for performance. Instead of focusing on the obvious issue of "Why is your pipeline not full?" she works with her team to brainstorm opportunities to generate more qualified leads. As a result, her team goes out with renewed enthusiasm and next week's scenario is almost always an improvement.

Celebrating successes not only cements positive self-belief but gives everyone a chance to learn from others and see what is possible. By bringing their toughest sales project to the table, sales reps get ideas and support on what can be done differently to improve results. "Often, as we are discussing one case, we'll realize that someone else also has the same issue and we can solve problems quickly. Everyone realizes that we are in this together and that creates a culture of empathy, camaraderie, and trust." says Lindsey.

The power of "why" and recognition

"When I took over the sales team," Kevin shared, "I had to understand what motivates each one on my team. Without knowing that it's hard to get your team to hit their targets. You can only push so hard at the end of the day, they have to want the success for themselves. My role as a manager is to find the 'why' and capitalize on that."

During goal-setting sessions with his team, Kevin keeps going back to their personal goals and their "why" for accomplishing the goal with his question, "If you achieved this, what would it mean for you personally?" Not only do they celebrate achievement of sales targets but they also celebrate personal accomplishments. Knowing what motivates his team allows Kevin to create opportunities for accomplishment. For instance, with one of his reps, Kevin realized that being in the lime light really motivated Janet. At the next regional sales monthly meeting, Kevin, had Janet present the team's results to the VP. When I met Janet a week later, I could see a difference in her energy and confidence level.

Step #6: Get your managers on the frontline

As part of the job description, you might want to have managers join reps on sales calls. There is no better way to understand what is really happening on the ground and stay in touch with the marketplace. Not only does your manager get to observe the reps' sales skills and provide feedback for improvement, but it is a valuable opportunity to gain insight into your customer's mind and great fodder for your next marketing campaign or product launch.

Step #7: Instill the value of accountability

When the need to be accepted is greater than the expectation of results, having your managers hold their teams accountable can be challenging. There are three key elements that play a pivotal role in helping your managers hold their team accountable:

1. Have a mindset for success. Expect the best from them and their teams, and don't let excuses get in the way of performance. That's why setting clear expectations, deliverables, and getting buy-in becomes key.

2. Managing by metrics alone will not lead to success. Managing behaviors is what determines success. When a manager or a salesperson doesn't do what they commit to, how do you address it?

3. The ability to have crucial conversations around performance and being able to give feedback in an objective manner without damaging relationships.

I was coaching a sales team in Kenya during the 2017 elections. Usually during elections, business activity slows down considerably. We knew this going into the year that the months leading up to the election would be slow and our buyers would use the uncertainty to defer purchases. Instead of accepting that this was just the way the market behaves, we focused on getting really good at handling what we called the "election objection." When we had clients tell us that they would wait for the election to make a decision, we countered with statistics and reports that showed prospective buyers how property values appreciated subsequent to every election and how they could benefit by buying now vs. later. We converted many a skeptic into buyers and had the best month right before elections. Not only that, for one of the products the team exceeded their 2017 targets by July, fifteen days before the election date.

It was not just the fact that we had done our homework. It began with the expectation of results and not buying into the "election objection" ourselves as a team. Both the sales manager and the team thought of possibilities and solutions instead of accepting the widely held belief that sales would be slow. The sales manager laid out expectations for goals very clearly and the team agreed on rules to differentiate a "genuine refusal from a prospect" vs. their inability to make a sale. It also meant that we had to be willing to hold people accountable for results and not buy into excuses. Along the way we had to make tough decisions and let two salespeople go.

Step #8: Implement and drive sales strategy

Making time to connect the strategy with day-to-day actions becomes key to staying focused on the game and ensuring that your strategy is implemented at the ground level. Often managers can be so caught up in the numbers game and meeting targets that it is easy to lose focus of the big picture.

Make strategy meetings a regular part of the role. Constant focus on the strategy ensures that the important stuff is not being forgotten. At one of the companies I advise, not only do they run through the weekly targets with their teams, but they have a discussion every 2–3 weeks on what changes are being noticed in the marketplace and how marketing campaigns are being implemented. Constant flow of insights between sales managers and their regional heads and country CEOs keeps the attention on the strategy and allows for adjustments to happen quickly.

Step #9: Manage pipelines proactively

Hopefully, your customer relationship management (CRM) reflects the stages in your sales process and is able to give you a fairly accurate projection of sales you can expect your team to produce. Even with the best CRMs in place, I find managers often struggling with the forecasted amount.

Here's a quick technique your sales manager can use to project sales numbers—and one that allows you to quickly check their revenue forecasts. I have a real estate client who has a sales goal of thirty properties every month, each amounting to $50,000. This means she needs $1.5 million per month in sales or thirty clients (assuming each client buys one property). An average closing rate for her team is 20%. So that means to get 30 clients, she needs to have 150 prospects in the pipeline:

$$\text{Business in pipeline} = \frac{\text{sales target}}{\text{closing \% or conversion rate of your team}}$$

$$\text{Business in pipeline} = \frac{30}{0.20}$$

$$= 150 \text{ prospects}$$

An average sale takes about ninety days to complete.

If her target for November is 1,500,000, that means she needs to have 150 prospects or 4,500,000 (150 × 30,000) in the pipeline by August to ensure November targets are met:

Sales cycle = 3 months

Date of goal − sales cycle = when your potential
business must be in
your pipeline

$$\frac{\text{November } 30 - 90 \text{ days}}{\text{(or 3 months)}} = \text{August } 31$$

If you know beforehand how much you will need each month to meet your numbers, it creates clarity around the activity needed. It also gives you a chance to recover when you are lagging behind on your numbers.

Your sales manager is a key implementer of your sales strategy. Are you maximizing the potential for your business from this position? The only way your manager can meet their targets is by helping each rep on their team to reach their targets. The more they focus on getting team members to succeed, the greater the results. It's the ability to lead and coach their teams and not the ability to land new opportunities or close business that will set them up for success.

Chapter summary

1. Be clear on the role of your sales manager—a sales manager achieves your sales targets by leveraging the strengths of each salesperson on their team.

2. Your best salesperson will not always be the best sales manager.

3. Look for the six key competencies and skills in your sales manager before you make a decision on whom to hire.

4. 70% of your sales manager's time needs to be allocated to coaching, managing pipelines, and selling.

5. Coaching impacts your bottom line positively. To win the game of sales, the focus has to be as much on the inner game as on the outer game.

6. Sales managers need to be self-aware to coach and motivate the team. They need to develop themselves to develop the team.

7. Get your managers on the frontline and out of the office. There is no better way to understand what is really happening on the ground and stay in touch with the marketplace.

8. Motivation doesn't come from a seminar. Build motivation into the daily routine through coaching, creating learning opportunities, and joint goal-setting.

9. Conduct sales meetings that motivate and focus on problem-solving instead of micro-management.

10. Your sales manager is a key implementer of your sales strategy. Get your managers to make time to connect the strategy with day-to-day actions to stay focused on sales instead of always being caught up in the numbers game.

7
The 80/20 Rule For Hiring The Right People

There's a Dakota American Indian saying that says, "When you discover you're riding a dead horse, the best strategy is to dismount." If you discovered you were riding a dead horse, you would think I was off my rocker if I were to suggest that perhaps buying a stronger whip, changing riders or rewriting the minimum performance requirements for the horse might improve the situation. But how often do we hold on to salespeople who won't perform despite more time, more product training, or more teamwork? How much time—and money—is invested in dead horses that do nothing but slow you down?

If somebody came to mind just now and the thought of that wasted money and effort makes you cringe, don't beat yourself up. You're not the first person to hang on to hope for an underperforming salesperson.

I once had a sales rep stay on with me for almost four months without once meeting her sales goals before I decided I needed to do something about it. Caroline came recommended from a business colleague and had been a good performer in her previous role. Not only did she have a good résumé, but she was confident during the interview process.

At the end of three months, she was lagging behind on her targets. Did this raise any red flags? Probably a small one in the back of my mind, which I chose to ignore because I was busy telling myself that it takes time, that Caroline was really just getting the hang of things. So I did what all smart business leaders do. I gave her some more time and waited for the results to show up.

Quite frankly, I had so much on my plate running my business at the time that I let the three-month deadline pass and just didn't want to deal with the situation. It hadn't yet reached crisis mode. Plus, it was reassuring to hear the old "I have this huge contract coming through any minute" sales story.

I should have known better, right? But I'm only human.

Redesign your hiring process

In the end, things didn't work out with Caroline, which is a shame. You might think it's cruel of me to refer to unproductive salespeople as "dead horses," but all I really mean is that she wasn't a good fit for our company. She had done a great job in her previous position, and perhaps she did well at her next company, too. She and I would have both been better off if I'd been wise enough to read the writing on the wall earlier.

We all want results, and it's comforting to believe that just because a salesperson has a great résumé and came across confident at the interview, he or she would make a great candidate. What is often at play here is what psychologist Edward Thorndike named the "halo effect."[23]

The halo effect refers to how people subconsciously bias themselves to like other people. In a hiring context, the halo effect often leads us to believe, "If I hire someone with great experience, they should have the same success rate with my products or services. After all, they seemed pretty confident at the interview."

We inherently desire to see the good in others, so we sometimes ignore otherwise obvious indicators to

---

23 Half R (2015) "Hiring and the Halo Effect." https://roberthalf.com. au/blog/hiring-and-halo-effect-trap

the contrary. Our job as interviewers is to look for the reasons for hiring them and the risks in doing so. The halo effect blinds us to the risk.

The good thing about the Caroline situation is that it taught me to be a little more empathetic toward my clients when they were faced with similar situations. Instead of giving them that condescending look of horror that screams, "How could you be so blind— why would you wait so long?" I now knew exactly what they were going through. It has also made me vigilant when it comes to biases, and it has changed the interviewing process with my clients so they don't fall prey to the halo effect.

The dreaded three-month waiting game

When I started working with Joseph, CEO of a CGI company in the US, he had an aggressive sales goal of $1 million per sales rep to meet to get to their annual targets. This also meant that he needed to hire four more sales reps who could get up to speed fast and start performing immediately. Joseph had been through the process of interviewing for some time, even hired two people, but was not happy with the results he was seeing.

"Could you take me through your hiring process?" I asked Joseph as we sat down to discuss a few hires that were giving him trouble.

"Well," Joseph said, "we placed an ad. I also asked my peers, and they sent me a few referrals. The résumés looked pretty good, and the interviews went well. Quite honestly, we were under a lot of pressure to grow the team quickly. I wanted to get the hiring done, start the product training, and have some time to breathe. Three months seemed like a pretty good period. We hired three people. They have been with us for four months now. I think one is a keeper for sure. I am not so sure about Frank. Maybe I need to give him some more time. As for Mike, I think I will have to let him go."

The phrase "give him some more time" sounded familiar to me, and the red flag was at full-mast this time.

Don't get me wrong. I think it is a good idea to give someone a ramp-up period if they are the right candidate. However, the downside is that it also takes three months to figure out if the candidate is really the right person for the job, which means you are already a quarter behind in your sales targets for the year if this person doesn't perform. That's exactly where Joseph found himself at the end of his hiring process.

I can't stress how much time, effort and money it will save if you invest just a little bit more time in the hiring process upfront instead of playing the three-month waiting game over and over again. After helping clients hire hundreds of salespeople, here are a few of the strategies I have found to reduce the risk of a bad hire.

Make your prospective candidates prove themselves before you even invite them to an interview

Hiring for a sales position is unlike hiring for any other position, and making your prospective new hires jump through a few hoops is not only healthy, it's crucial. Let's face it, your customers will make your salespeople jump through hoops every single day! In fact, when salespeople try to sell to you, you probably put them through multiple hoops before you even agree to give them a meeting, right? So why should it be different when it comes to hiring your own salespeople?

In Joseph's case, we changed his hiring process a bit. Instead of scanning through almost a hundred résumés, we did this instead: When we received a résumé, we sent an email thanking the candidate for applying and asking them to call in at a particular time on a certain date and leave a voicemail. We also asked them to send an email response to three questions.

Here were some of the interesting observations gained from the process:

- **Not everyone's heart was in it.** One-third of the candidates did not bother calling back.

- **Simple directions proved too complicated for some of them.** There were about fifteen candidates who called back at a later time and made excuses for why they couldn't call earlier. Some didn't call but emailed their responses instead. This revelation provided valuable insight, as this is exactly the kind of salesperson you probably don't want on your team. If a prospect asks them to call back at a certain time, rest assured they are not going to be the ones responding to the request.

- **Screening candidates became much easier.** One interesting question we asked was, "What frustrated you most about your last job?" This provided interesting responses to say the least. By reading their messages, you could tell if they took responsibility for their own actions or put the blame squarely on the economy, market conditions or their boss.

Bonus: It took only an hour to sort through the twenty recorded messages and select the candidates for the next step versus spending hours going through a hundred résumés that didn't even warrant an initial look.

Try the group audition approach vs. the individual interview approach

The next step in the process is to invite the candidates that made it through the hoops to a group audition. All candidates were invited for the audition on the same day and informed that they would be interviewing alongside other candidates. If the *American Idol* audition comes to mind and makes you raise your eyebrows, relax, it's not that sort of an audition I am talking about.

First things first, let me take you through what this group audition looks like so we are on the same page. A group of five to eight candidates are invited to the session. Three or four representatives from your company form the interview team.

Introductions

As candidates come in introductions are made, a quick company tour given, and even refreshments served. Why, you ask? The answer is three-fold. First, for the candidates to open up and be themselves so you can learn more about them. The more they talk the more insight you get into how they think. Second, you get to see how these candidates network with others and engage you. These will be the people representing your company and you want to know upfront how well they can engage with your customer. It also tells you how quickly they adapt to an unfamiliar situation. All of these are important traits that you want in your sales team.

The questions round

Once Joseph and his team were done with the introductions, here's what happened next. The group audition began with an overview of the company, vision, mission and culture. One of the team members shared their experience of working in the company so that candidates got an understanding of what life here looks like. Then began the "questions round." (You can choose to ask four or five questions that give you an insight into candidates' selling styles.) The same question was posed to all the candidates and each candidate had to respond. Usually I also like to hear their one-minute pitch, eg name, what makes them a great sales professional, what do they bring to the table.

Why do this? Because you want to know how they would interact in a networking event, wouldn't you? Can they really use this opportunity to articulate what they bring to the table?

Of course, consider a round-robin approach, where you don't always start and end with the same person. Give all the interviewers in your team a chance to ask questions to break the monotony. You also want to make sure that everyone on your interview team gets a chance to observe how the candidates respond to questions. You will be surprised at what your team picks up from the answers.

As candidates respond to questions and share their responses with the entire audience, you get a feel for their confidence level, communication and presentation skills. What is interesting is that you can tell a lot about a person when you watch them interact with others, much more than the typical résumé line "I am a great communicator." Guess what? You just have to see it "live" for yourself. Now you can choose to believe what's on the résumé or decide for yourself. Another thing that is interesting is how other candidates are responding when someone is speaking. Their body language and level of interest also tells you about their listening skills. It is also a good way to assess who thinks outside the box when responding to a question or whether they tend to follow the same pattern as the first person who started out.

Questions to ask in a group audition

Interviewing salespeople is a tad different than interviewing for other positions. Salespeople interact with people all day and they are used to coming up with creative answers or answers that their prospects would like to hear. Of course they are going to take that approach with you in the interviews. When you present them with a hypothetical question, such as, "How would you deal with a customer that wants a huge discount?" they'll tell you what you want to hear, which is, "I don't like to do that, but show them the benefits instead."

If you have been using traditional interview techniques and asking questions such as "What motivates you?" or "What are your strengths and weaknesses?" then it's probably time to ditch these questions.

Imagine what the person sitting across from you is thinking as you ask these questions. "Ok I am looking for better pay but I am not going to tell you that," or "I am really bad at following up with a prospect but there is no way I am going to tell you that."

Instead, the answers will probably sound more like this: "Oh, I am looking for something that challenges me," or "I am not that strong at organization," which you can interpret as "my notes are all over the place and I have no system for following up on my prospect."

As often as these questions are used, they don't tell you much because the answers to them are often vague and give people a chance to hide behind them. Moreover, the answers are rehearsed. If you Google the answers to these questions, I guarantee you will have a good laugh. Lastly, it's hard to relate an answer like "challenging" to a job skill. Is that a requirement for the job? What you probably want from this person is persistence.

How do you get around that and understand more about this person's selling style?

Competency or behavioral-based interviewing techniques. What does this mean? The idea is to assess how someone would demonstrate certain behaviors and skills in this position. Examples of how you dealt with situations in the past is a fairly good determinant of how you would perform in these situations in the future.

For instance, if you want to assess if your future sales-person knows how to negotiate, which is a key skill for the job, you might ask her a question like this:

"Tell me about a situation when your client insisted on a better deal than you were offering."

Since this question asks your candidate to elaborate on their past experiences, it's hard to invent a story on your feet. Your brain's first response to this question is to search through your memory files and present you with similar experiences. Of course, your candidate can still be vague and avoid sharing details, but to drill down and find out if they are being evasive, ask them: "What, specifically, did you do in this situation? What were some of the actions you took? What challenges did you encounter? And what was the result?" This approach is also referred to as the STAR (situation, task, action, result) model. Questions like these give you an opportunity to assess if your candidate has the key competencies or skills that are going to be important in this position.

Assess sales effectiveness correctly

In other words, what are the skills, behaviors and knowledge that are required for high performance in a particular sales role? Also known as core competencies for a role. By focusing on the core competencies, it is much easier to set and measure performance expectations for a role. Sales effectiveness is not just a function of how well your sales executive sells but also depends on your product, sales strategy, your market, and how your customers like to buy. For instance, if you are in the business of selling auto-insurance, your sales rep needs to be really good at selling on the phone and closing a sale quickly. The sales skills that are required to sell a low-level insurance product will be very different to how you might sell an ERP system, for that matter.

Let's break this down. How do you ascertain whether a candidate will be effective? First, we need to understand what tasks must be performed to succeed in this role and how they will be accomplished. In other words, do they have the skill and knowledge to do it? For instance, if we need sales reps to sell an ERP system, do they have a basic knowledge and understanding of what an ERP system entails? Do they have strong consultative sales skills to diagnose an organization's primary issues with their IT and work like an advisor? What behaviors will be necessary to accomplish these tasks? If you are selling ERP systems, a key behavior is how well the salesperson follows up and keeps the prospect engaged. As you design the hiring process and interview questions, you need to understand the sales competencies you need for the role.

I like to use the list of key sales tasks and behaviors listed in The Profile Sales Assessment by Profiles International as a starting point and guide:[24]

---

24 See www.profilesinternational.com/Select-and-Motivate-Sales-Stars. aspx

The Profiles International Profiles Sales Assessment

Key tasks	Behaviors required
Prospecting	Creativity and flexibility in looking for leads, energy level in pursuing prospects—eg level of reluctance with cold calling, motivation to continue activity
Closing the sale	Confidence, assertiveness, perseverance, qualification of needs, decisiveness
Prioritization	Decisiveness, level of manageability needed, independence
Taking initiative	Objective judgment
Building relationships	Social interactions, outgoing, friendly, co-operative, agreeable
Working with a team	Co-operation, co-ordination, competitiveness
Learning agility	Ability to learn from mistakes, synthesize new information

What does this mean for the interviewing process and questions?

Once you have identified the sales tasks and behaviors needed to assess sales effectiveness, your interview questions will be designed to get an insight into these skills and behaviors.

Always ask the right questions

If you want to understand how well a sales rep prospects, here are some questions you can use to ascertain their ability to prospect.

Key sales task: prospecting

Assessing skills:

- Tell me about your best strategy for getting leads.
- What did you say in your cold call to get the prospect to meet with you?

Assessing behavior:

- Tell me about a time when you had to quickly fill your pipeline. What did you do?

Key sales task: learning agility

Assessing skills:

- How do you keep up with the trends in your marketplace?
- What kind of research do you do before you meet with a prospect?

Assessing behavior:

- What did you learn from the last sale you didn't close?

Key sales task: closing the sale

Assessing skills:

- What do you do to ensure that you have the best chance of closing a sale?

Assessing behavior:

- Tell me about a time when prospects told you that they needed time to think about your product and how you turned the situation around.
- What was the toughest sales situation you had to deal with and how did you manage to get the prospect on board?

Now that you have asked these questions, what happens after the group audition?

At the end of the group audition, which took about 90 minutes, Joseph and his team thanked all the candidates for coming and informed them that they would be contacted within a few days. After the candidates left, it was time for a debrief and a discussion of everyone's top three candidates with an explanation of why they made the list. You couldn't just say "I liked that person," but had to fill in with specific examples such as, "I liked the way Mark talked about his experience in the negotiation situation, and told us how he designed a spreadsheet that showed the prospect all three scenarios and why the current pricing was a good deal. I think that was persuasive and creative. We need salespeople who are persuasive and don't give in to our clients all the time."

By eliminating the subjectivity, focusing on facts, and listening to what other interviewers had picked out in the conversations, the team was able to pick their top three candidates for the final interviews.

The final one-on-one interview stage

You can use more of the behavioral-based questions to dig deep. What I find to be even more useful in the sales interview is the "sell me" approach. Not the sell me the pen video that you have seen multiple times on YouTube. I am not a big fan of that because the candidate is working on a hypothetical situation, doesn't know anything about the product and spends most of their time making it up as they go. I find that a better approach is to get them to sell their current product to you. First it tells you how well they know their product, how passionate they are about it and how well they handle objections and ask for the sale. Seriously, if they can't do all this with the current product that they have been selling for the past two years, what makes you think they'll do justice to your product?

Joseph picked two out of the three candidates he invited in the one-on-one interview based on how well they sold to him.

Sales assessments—save time and money

My mentor Andrew Priestley gave me this great piece of advice regarding what to say when his clients ask him about the importance of assessments: "Would you buy a car without taking a test drive?"

The obvious answer for anyone is a resounding, "No!" So why would you hire a salesperson for three months and pay them a salary without knowing whether they can sell? Get the point?

The purpose of sales assessments is to give you an objective look at the behaviors and motivations of your salespeople so that you can make better decisions when it comes to hiring, managing, and developing them.

One of my clients decided to hire an individual who scored low on "independence" (a sub-category within the Prioritization section of the Sales Assessment Profile). Her low score in this category implied that she would hesitate when making decisions on her own. As they further explored this with the candidate, it turned out that she simply liked to have the right information before she rushed into a decision. Low independence in this situation could be managed easily. Because the company was in a transition stage, phasing out old products and launching new ones, it was important that the candidate check in with the sales manager if she was unsure on an area.

The cost vs. the benefits

If you find yourself asking, "How much do these assessments cost? They must be expensive!" I would suggest you consider the math. Sales assessments usually range from $150 to $300. If you paid your salesperson a monthly salary of $3,000–$5,000 per month over the course of that dreaded three-month waiting period, only to discover they didn't measure up, you would spend $15,000 only to start your search for the right candidate all over again. And just imagine if you pay them more per month that that. You can't tell me that $150 to $300 spent up front can possibly compare to three months' wages. Something to think about.

I really like the Profiles International Sales Assessment. You can check it out at www.profilesinternational.com and request sample reports.

The goal of the sales assessment is to give you an insight into the strengths of the salesperson and if they were to join, what you would need to know from a development and management perspective. You cannot use the assessment alone as a basis for not taking someone on board, as that goes against HR polces on discrimination.

Lastly, let your HR people complete the internal hiring process with reference and background checks before you make a final offer.

Try the three-pronged approach. I am not saying that this a fool-proof method to hiring, but it definitely works better than the traditional hiring process when it comes to sales. No, there is no silver bullet, but wouldn't you rather find out at the beginning rather than later?

It is hard to predict with 100% accuracy if your new hire is going to be a stellar salesperson. After all, we are all human. But at least you would have done everything in your power to reduce the risk. One thing is for sure: the pressure of resurrecting the dead horse is over.

Chapter summary

1. While it's a great idea to give people a ramp-up period, it's even better to invest in the hiring process upfront. That way the three months is a valuable learning period, not a wasted quarter.

2. There's a proven process for hiring the best sales candidates and it's not the same as hiring other positions. Feel free to adapt some of the ideas from our unique hiring process.

3. Try the group audition approach vs. the individual interview approach.

4. When assessing sales effectiveness, look at both the sales tasks that must be performed to succeed in this role and the behaviors needed to accomplish that.

5. Your interview questions should be designed to get an insight into the candidate's skills and behaviors relevant to the sales tasks.

6. Don't skimp on sales assessments, because they'll save you money in the long run. The purpose of sales assessments is to give you an objective look at the behaviors and motivations of your salespeople so that you can make better decisions when it comes to hiring, managing, and developing them.

FACTOR THREE

SALES AGILITY—TRAIN FOR PERFORMANCE

8
Create A Culture
Of Learning

M ore than ever, learning agility—or how fast one learns and applies new skills and adapts to changing situations—determines one's success as a sales leader and a salesperson. Your customers' needs are constantly changing in response to the marketplace. There is more competition than ever before in the marketplace and instant gratification is an expectation.

The question is, how do you keep up with this?

Investing in your sales team's skills is not a one-off but an ongoing exercise in continuous improvement. Just as you are always improving your products or spending money on R&D, your salespeople must be as proficient in their ability to articulate the value you have to offer to customers and match their needs to your products.

As customers, we don't need salespeople. We need experts who will partner with us in the buying process and empower us to sift through the data and make sense of it to make the right decision.

With that in mind, are your salespeople walking in as the expert ready to provide value or just looking to close a deal? The answer to that question determines your approach to the training program you put in place.

What does a good training program need to have?

A salesperson's ability to sell depends on their ability to prospect, sell and convey a value proposition in a manner that appeals to the customers. In essence, this forms the foundation of the program. Sales skills take time to master and develop. Getting your team in a one-day or two-day training once or twice a year is not going to achieve your objectives. If you're truly looking for transformation, then design your sales program in accordance with the sales competencies, tasks, and behaviors you have identified as essential for success.

Skills development

Look at the development plans for your sales team and incorporate skill areas in the program that will make an impact on the skill level. Competency is a result of sales skills and applying the behavior to master the skill.

Empowering behaviors

Your program needs to look at incorporating the behavior element. For example, if you're looking for your reps to be more confident in handling sales objections, you need to: a) address their beliefs about objections, b) teach them how to apply techniques to counter an objection, and c) help them develop empowering habits or routines to maintain a positive outcome.

The Be × Do = Have formula:

Be (personal development or beliefs about objections) × Do (skills in applying the techniques)

= Have (proficiency in sales)

Without including an element of personal development or focusing on the BE, sales transformation is not possible.

A clearly defined process

Another area that is crucial to consider is where in the sales process your sales reps get stuck and what skills are needed to move the sale forward. Skills training without an understanding of process, structure or strategy is not good enough.

Is your sales training still relevant?

When was the last time your training team designed the curriculum in the context of your sales strategy, new products, sales team's development plans or current market conditions? I am not asking you to reinvent the wheel but make sure that the original training addresses real-life challenges your sales team is dealing with today. I frequently come across scripts and guides that were designed a while back to meet a certain challenge, but the issue is no longer relevant.

The importance of effective application

If your sales training is not a "simulation of real-life problem-solving" or akin to a "war room session" where your focus is on applying new techniques to penetrate a market/account or proactively preventing roadblocks even before they occur, then it may be time to reconsider the effectiveness of your sales training programs.

Adult learning happens through application. One area I like to incorporate is "hot seats," where sales reps submit a pressing problem they are facing and are open to being coached to solve it for themselves. Not only does that give them their own insights but brainstorming as a group opens up a whole new possibility of solutions. Oftentimes as we are tackling a situation with one sales rep, it ends up benefiting many more people who are facing the same dilemma.

In one situation, a rep was dealing with a very tough sale. Not only did we work on the initial sales call but walked through the whole sales process and dealt with hurdles that might come up so that they were better prepared to deal with all possibilities when they left the room.

Unless you can understand and relate to the real-life problems salespeople are facing in selling it's hard to come up with solutions that matter to them. A salesperson hates nothing more than spending a day not making money. If your training will make them money, they will stay on.

Should you have in-house trainers, or should you hire external companies?

There are pros and cons to both options. While in-house trainers may have a good knowledge of your company, outside trainers bring an outsider's perspective to your team which is often beneficial as it keeps the focus on the customer.

No matter where they come from, the main thing I would recommend is that the person training your team should always be someone who has sold for a living. You can't teach sales if you have never sold before, just as you cannot be in charge of leading a sales team if you haven't sold before. Unless you have personally been stumped by a client's question, fumbled at objections, lost your voice making a cold call, and experienced the pain of losing a sale, you cannot relate to what your audience is going through, and will not be able to help them.

I was humbled when the sales director of my banking client came to me after one of the sessions on objection handling and told me, "You handled the objection better than any of our relationship managers can do, and they are the experts in that product."

Does your sales manager have to be present for training sessions?

"Lead by example" is the first rule of leadership. As the leader of the pack, your sales managers need to be engaged in the training program. They will be fascinated about what they find out about their sales team. Especially as the team goes through role-plays and some tough scenarios. They get a first-hand experience of how prepared their sales team really is and how skills are applied in a real-life context. It's also a great platform for managers to share their insights and experience in a way that is better received, and creates empathy and understanding of what each side faces.

I remember during one of my training sessions, the manager put herself out there for an "objection handling" exercise. She had a fairly new team and they were having a tough time dealing with objections. She volunteered to be the sales rep and her sales reps got to be tough clients who kept giving her objections as she dealt with each one.

Watching her confidence and style of handling these objections was a great learning experience for the team. When she messed up, she was brave enough to laugh at herself and ask for help. Not only did she earn newfound respect among her team for her willingness to put herself out there and learn from her mistakes but it went a long way in establishing a learning culture for her team.

Shared experiences create team alignment and team cohesiveness. During training, shift happens and your attitude as a manager might be just what is needed to propel someone in the direction of reaching their potential. This could never have been achieved had she chosen to remain in her office.

Prepare new reps to hit the ground running

"We have a new team joining us and they need to catch up with the rest of the team. Should we have a week of sales training in the beginning to have them caught up?" asked Jane, the sales manager.

While it is really tempting to do this, don't overload new employees with all the product information and sales training in one go, as 80% of all that stuff is going to evaporate as soon as they leave the room. Instead, spread it over a longer period of time so that they have a continuous support system.

In Jane's case, I suggested, "I think it will be best if they implement one skill at a time so they are able to see how it works and retain that experience. Also, at this point, it is a case of 'I don't know what I don't know.' Unless they implement the techniques and make their own mistakes they will not retain the information."

Here are a few suggestions to incorporate in your on-boarding program to quickly upskill your new reps:

1. Practice, practice and practice. One way to quickly increase reps' product knowledge is to get them to present a product to the team during a team meeting and handle objections.

2. Have new reps tag-team with one of your senior reps on a sales call.

3. Get your managers to debrief sales calls with new reps immediately afterward, when the conversation is still fresh.

4. Let new reps do a sales demo with you before the sales call.

5. Create feedback loops in the training program that focus on how well reps implement a particular skill and give suggestions for improvement.

6. Pair them with a sales coach for improved performance.

7. Don't just set reps sales goals but review their plan of action with them beforehand. That way you can foresee and solve problems together, instead of going down a rabbit hole.

It's not just for the newbies

When new sales reps come on board, they usually have to go through an initial training to get them up to speed with the industry, products, and customer problems.

Over time, it's only natural for sales reps who have been selling for a long time to get caught up in the "I know" cycle. I had the director of commercial banking tell me at the end of the training, "We had a few senior sales reps wondering why they should be in the training since they are so good at what they do. But interestingly enough, they told me how glad they were to come here today." The best of us forget. It's about consistently sharpening our saw, especially in a world that is changing so fast. Learning never stops in sales.

Leverage your service and support teams for sales

We have talked about the importance of letting salespeople sell without bogging them down with support functions and restructuring the sales process to enable them to focus on delivering a stellar experience to their customers.

Your service team interacts as much with your customers if not the same as your sales team. Investing in training your service team at a level that the sales team is trained at ensures that there is a consistent experience for the client. Not only that, because the service teams are directly supporting the sales staff in many instances, they can expedite the sales cycle time by being a key point of contact for the customer. In addition, because the service team is already familiar with customers' needs and products, it's easy for them to spot opportunities for additional sales at the back end and offer salespeople key insights.

A great example is how a banking client rewards their customer service team for regularly sharing insights with their sales teams. Customer service reps get recognized for their role in growing an existing account and also receive a bonus. By working as one team, not only can customer problems be resolved quickly but there is a motivation to get it done right and work more cohesively as a team.

Build learning agility daily

Training and learning does not stop after the training session. Here are some ways you can ensure that this becomes part of everyday life.

Weekly sales meetings

Meetings should emphasize problem-solving vs. status reports. The primary purpose of meetings has somehow been relegated to reporting on activity levels that nobody looks forward to and drags down everyone. The effectiveness of sales meetings can be maximized when you turn it into a forum for problem-solving and get your team to actively contribute their insights.

For example, the sales meeting at one of my clients has taken a whole new turn where everyone actually looks forward to it. After a quick update on numbers, the team members focus on four main areas:

1. Networking: asking group members for any help with introductions into a company they might be targeting.

2. Preparing for an upcoming sales meeting and/or asking for insights.

3. Sharing their most important lesson from a sale they closed or didn't close.

4. Sharing new information: Some of the new information gathered over the past week might be beneficial to the entire group. By integrating this into their existing process, learning has become an everyday practice.

Reminders to focus on skill improvement during monthly goal-setting sessions

Often when we set sales goals, we take a look at the strategies and tactics to get there. Seldom do we focus on integrating skills improvement in the plan. For example, if one of the goals is to bring in five new accounts this month, we look at prospecting strategies such as networking, LinkedIn, email prospecting, etc. To successfully implement each one of the strategies, you also have to get better at executing each one of these areas. For example, email prospecting is not going to work as well for you, if you don't know how to write emails that get attention and have a strong call to action. One of the goals that is also important to set as you determine your strategy is skills improvement goals. How are you going to learn to improve your email prospecting skills? Do you need to study copywriting skills or understand how to create an email sequence?

The 21-day habit strategy to implement a skill

A key element of our training programs involves implementing a 21-day skill challenge. In one of my recent training sessions on cold calling, the team committed to a 21-day challenge to apply the script they created. When we got back for our next session, we reviewed what was working well for the team and identified any areas of challenge. It was very interesting to see the energy in the room. People were exchanging notes on what worked, how they overcame some of the objections and gained new insights from each other. We had a few good laughs on the mess ups and what not to do next time.

By acknowledging the mistakes and turning it into a positive learning experience, it allowed people to connect at a much deeper level with each other and imbibe the lessons. At the end of the exercise you could see a determination to move to the next level.

Integrating across geographical areas

An area that I have found works really well as I work with teams that are geographically dispersed in different parts of the world is delivering my training in short video messages. During one session, we were working through the sales introduction pitch. As part of the exercise, each person had to record their pitch and send it over for review.

With technology you can get as creative as you want. It doesn't always have to be in the classroom. Through webinars we run group coaching calls and can still run hot seat sessions.

In the next chapter we're going to look at how your sales team interacts with the customer, and those vital touchpoints on the customer's journey.

Chapter summary

1. How fast one learns and applies new skills and adapts to changing situations determines one's success as a salesperson. Investing in your sales team's skills is not a one-time exercise but an ongoing exercise in continuous improvement. Just as you are always improving your products or spending money on R&D, your salespeople must be as proficient in their ability to articulate the value you have to offer to customers and match their needs to your products.

2. Training is not a one-off exercise—you need to inculcate a process of continuous learning and improvement.

3. Don't take it for granted that your current sales training program is fit for purpose. Ensure that your sales training is aligned with your sales strategy, their personal development and current market conditions.

4. Develop a great training plan, that you can effectively apply, related to real-life problems your salespeople will face.

5. To embed the learning culture, meet regularly to solve problems together.

9

Deliver A Phenomenal Sales Experience

Customer service experience gets a whole lot of press and attention as being key to customer retention and referrals. Absolutely true. But guess where the customer experience starts? First contact with your company, and that first contact is frequently your sales team.

This is a vital truth, because it means that something as seemingly minor as how your salesperson answers a phone call or responds to an email sets the tone of the entire sales experience for the prospect—and determines whether they will move forward.

The close of the sale starts with first contact and continues all the way through to delivery of the service and receiving referrals. It doesn't end with signing a contract.

According to the Disney Institute, "Customer experience is the sum of all interactions a customer has with a company."[25] Every touchpoint in your sales process either enhances the customer experience or negates it.

But not much thought is given to how to start a relationship on the right foot when the prospect first engages with the company. The experience at the time of engagement is most often left in the hands of the salesperson. It is generally assumed that they will do what is necessary in getting the relationship to a close. That is a great assumption and even accountants recognize client lunches as a deductible expense. It's great if you have a good salesperson who is naturally skilled at building client relationships. However, usually that's where it stops. But even with the best of salespeople, life gets in the way and there are too many leads to follow up on and deliver a stellar sales experience.

Why is the sales experience important, you ask? Because your prospect buys two things from you: your service and the experience of doing business with you. I will cover this in more detail when we get to the

---

25 CX Journey (2018) "Customer Experience and Customer Service: What's the difference?" www.cx-journey.com/2018/10/customer-experience-and-customer.html

referrals section. People buy on emotion and justify with logic. According to Harvard Business School professor Gerald Zaltman, "95% of our purchase decisions take place in the subconscious mind."[26] "We reach a conclusion based on our emotional response and then support it with a logical reason."[27]

Step into the shoes of your customer for a few minutes and picture exactly how you would like YOUR business to treat YOU. What do you want to feel when you call or walk in? How would you like to be greeted? What experience do you want to leave with?

Secondly if you leave the sales experience to the salesperson entirely, things will be forgotten. Success is a result of both process and people; have the process support the work your sales team does, and you will see big differences.

---

26   Mahoney, M (2003) "The Subconscious Mind of the Consumer (And How To Reach It)." https://hbswk.hbs.edu/item/the-subconscious-mind-of-the-consumer-and-how-to-reach-it
27   Business.com (2015) "Facts Vs. Emotions: When to Use Each Tactic to Make a Sale." https://business.com/articles/facts-vs-emotions-when-to-use-each-tactic-to-make-a-sale

Four steps to build an incredible customer experience into your sales process

Step #1: Prioritize customer experience

Create a vision of perfection centered on the prospect

What do you want to share with your prospects when they call or walk in or visit your website? I was mystery shopping a client who is in the luxury golf estate business. They spend a considerable amount of money on making sure that their website, marketing materials, and press releases reflect the brand they want to convey. It all looked great on paper until I picked up the phone and talked with one of their salespeople. She was professional, gave me the information, and asked me to come down for the tour.

During the sales tour I got a good look at the properties I was interested in and was given all the pertinent information. But there was a huge disconnect. The sales tour reflected nothing of the warmth, exclusivity, and the emotions their website and the brochures inspired.

You know the feeling you get when you visit a hospital? Sterile and efficient, but no warmth. Your sales process can feel like that to clients sometimes. You might be taking them through all the right steps and through the motions, but there is no connection. Sales is about connection.

Of course, you could argue that the salesperson in question just needed to do a better job. I'm tempted to agree with you; this salesperson was certainly not skilled in sales. But the fact is, the sales process did not support the sale, either.

Fixing this issue in your company begins with identifying what you want your prospect to feel at the end of the process. Sure, they may buy, but are they pulling their hair out by the time they're done?

Build emotional touchpoints

Your sales process probably has a few key steps mapped out such as:

- Prospecting (looking for new prospects)

- Connect with them via phone, email, or a meeting to gather more information or determine if they are a viable prospect

- Research their company and their needs

- Present your product or solution to them in a presentation

- Close the sale (this might include presenting a proposal, negotiation, getting a buy-in from all decision makers, and securing a signed agreement or contract)

When you look at these steps, they are very much about the process and can feel very transactional. Notice they are logical, but they don't inspire any emotion. It's the sterile hospital all over again.

I want to shift gears here a little bit and bring your competition into the picture for a moment. Your competitors also have a sales process, which most likely resembles yours. Your customer probably has done their research and figured out the benefits of both your company and your competition, and the only questions left to ask is, "Who do I buy from?"

The question you should be asking in response is, "How can we help them decide?" You help your prospects decide by making the experience memorable for them. This is achieved by inserting emotional touchpoints in your process.

Let's say one of the things you talk about in your marketing is your great service or how you are always there for your customers. How can that be reflected simply in your sales process? For instance, great service can be as simple as sending out a thank you card after the first meeting. It's as easy as that!

Creating an experience doesn't have to be expensive, and simple things can be very effective. Build in "send a thank you card" as an official step in your sales process for the salesperson to follow. Another idea could be sending out an industry article or resource that educates your client on how to solve their specific issue even before you meet with them the first time. What you add to your process is totally up to your creativity. The important point is having steps in place that generate the feelings you want to transfer to your client.

Amend your sales process and build touchpoints that build connections and make the clients feel valued every step of the way.

Step #2: Establish a clear hand-off

"Well, right now, our salesperson is the primary point of contact. Technically, even though the operations team takes it from here, the salesperson is still the point of contact in the relationship."

Does this sound familiar to you?

In regard to this issue, a sales rep once told me, "As the point of contact with the customer, it seems like we become the bad guys when something goes wrong internally. Ops is always getting on our case to deliver the bad news to the client. If documents aren't signed or payment forms aren't collected, we end up having to take care of that."

I titled this step "Establish a clear hand-off," but a suitable alternative title could have been "Transfer the relationship!" I understand that the salesperson is responsible for the relationship with the client, no two ways about it. But what happens gradually is that admin demands start to creep up from both the client and the internal departments, and sales reps find themselves in the position of dealing with issues they have no business dealing with. The more time they spend on admin work and/or putting out fires, the less time they have for making sales. An hour of admin time means that thirty prospect calls don't get made.

So, how can you fix this?

Define the last step in the sales process and clearly communicate it

Often, there is no clear transition from the sales process to the operations process, and the lines are blurred as to where sales stops and ops takes over. Most CRMs will identify that. But it begins with deciding on where the sales process stops. Establish a clear hand-off process from sales to operations.

For one of our clients, we introduced a formal "hand-off" step in the sales process where the salesperson formally introduced the ops person to the customer in person or via a conference call. During the meeting, the salesperson gave an overview of what to expect and how the job would progress to completion, then positioned the ops person as an expert. Here's how that looked:

"I am bringing Diana in because she is the expert of this stage and can answer your questions immediately with better information than I may have. I can certainly get you all the information you need, but I don't want you waiting on me to get back with the right information and be the bottleneck. I want you to have access to what you need immediately so we can help you move forward with the process. I will be on top of everything you need from our end and will be cc'd in all the communications. You have my contact information, so please reach out to me at any time if there is an issue. But knowing Diana, you probably will not need that."

The ops person then took over and shared a plan that detailed all the steps that would happen from this stage, along with timelines. In addition, she also set expectations for communication and defined the backup plan in case anything went wrong.

Just using this simple step has saved many of my clients from having their sales reps caught up in the admin loop and never being able to get out. The most important aspect of the transition is not about moving the client from one step of the process to the other but rather managing the relationship at every point. Your process is there to support the client experience and not just to push clients through the assembly line. One of the worst situations I came across was seeing a payment reminder letter sent out from the accounting department to clients. These letters almost sounded threatening in terms of imposing fines, when clearly the client was waiting on the company to deliver on a promise before their next payment. Leaving the relationship and emotional experience out of the process has disastrous effects on the overall customer experience and future business.

Step #3: Let salespeople sell

A less polite version of this title is: "Stop asking your sales staff to do admin stuff!"

Salespeople are eager to close the sale and sometimes will take it upon themselves to run the show, which is great initiative. But then they end up in account management rather than selling! Or perhaps the expectation is that for the salary that they earn, they should get some admin stuff done.

Let me invite you to evaluate the issue from an ROI perspective.

Say your top sales producer brings in $1 million in sales per month. That means her time is worth about $5,773 per hr. ($1 million / [4.33 weeks × 40 hours] = $5,773/hr.) You've heard the saying "time is money," right? Well, I don't think this statement is truer for any other profession than sales.

Now, would you rather have your top producer, who brings the company $5,773/hr., focus on sales (eg, prospecting, meeting clients, preparing proposals) or on filling out forms and doing paperwork to make your process smoother—tasks you could hire somebody to do for $20/hr.?

A great exercise to see how much this is costing your business in revenue is to find out what percentage of time your salespeople actually spend prospecting and selling vs. doing paperwork. In a sales productivity survey of 127 sales and marketing executives carried out by Docurated,[28] sales reps spent in excess of over 20% of their time on admin and paperwork, one-third on creating content or marketing material, and only one-third of their time actually selling.

If your sales reps are spending an average of 20% of their week on admin duties, that is time taken away from selling. Would you be better off having a sales rep, who normally closes sales of $1 million per month, increase their sales time by 20%? Or would you be better off saving a few dollars by having them do their own paperwork? ($20 × 8 hours per week admin time × 4.33 weeks = $692/month.)

If your sales reps are spending anything less than 50% of their time selling, it may be time to look at getting support staff to take over the admin responsibilities that have crept into the sales role. Let your sales reps

---

28   Brudner, E (2015, updated 2017) "Salespeople Only Spent One-Third of Their Time Selling Last Year [Infographic]." https://blog.hubspot.com/sales/salespeople-only-spent-one-third-of-their-time-selling-last-year

focus on building relationships and selling instead of sitting behind their desks.

Let your sales reps sell and let your support staff be support staff. In the long run, you will save money and time.

Step #4: Consider the big picture of product delivery

Your sales process is part of the larger picture of end-to-end delivery of your product; the experience you create is only part of the delivery of the final promise to your customer. Even though your sales process may end with the sales rep passing the baton on to the customer, the final promise to the customer doesn't stop here. A good sales process will not make up for an inefficient delivery process.

I was in a training session with a sales team that was blowing their numbers with one product but couldn't meet their numbers for another product that made 30% of their total target. Here was one of the challenges that came up in the conversation:

"We really aren't selling this product because we know it has operational challenges." I could sense a lot of hesitation.

"What's going on with that?" I asked.

"Well we haven't met the timelines that were promised to clients. I personally don't believe that we can deliver this project by August or next year. I had a prospect buy and then cancel the agreement. I know management wants us to keep pushing with sales. We have a meeting next week and the numbers aren't looking good."

If you don't believe in a product, it's very hard to sell it because your own doubts and objections get in the way. Instead of pushing the sales team for numbers, it might be time to look at your delivery of the product instead.

"How many prospects dropped out after signing the agreement because the project was delayed?" I asked. We went around the room and did the math. Sales revenue lost as a result of cancelled agreements amounted to $4.1 million.

"We worked hard to get that in the door and lost it because of operations. This is really not a sales issue. We would be on target with sales had we just kept the business. We have lost not only the business but the opportunity for referrals, and jeopardized our relationships."

I asked her to share the facts with the CEO. Facts have the power of getting you heard and takes the subjectivity out of the conversation. Sure enough, the numbers got the CEO's attention to expedite the process with the operations team and make the changes to the product.

How could we resolve this issue?

The product delivery cycle

By looking at the sales process in the context of the whole delivery cycle and involving both marketing and operations in problem-solving. We mapped out the entire process from lead generation to delivery of the product to streamline the process and cut out time and inefficiencies.

When everyone looked at the process in its entirety (not just their department) and from the perspective of the customer, they understood why each department was up in arms and what was at stake when one area could not deliver on the promise. These key questions took center stage:

1. Does this step add value to the client?

2. What problems could get in the way and how would we solve them before they even occurred?

Each department was forthcoming with ideas on how to prevent the problem instead of waiting until the end to solve a crisis. We left the meeting with an action plan and agreement in terms of responsibilities and actions.

As a result, sales were in a better position to set expectations correctly, anticipate what could go wrong and prepare for it beforehand. Sales also carried a clear hand-off to operations while they provided timelines and monitored the delivery process. Marketing was able to change the messaging and put together a set of FAQs to address objections prospects may have at the beginning.

Improve customer-centricity with these four ideas

Reviewing and adapting your sales process is part of the solution to creating a customer-centric sales process. Equally important is proactively bringing focus and mindfulness to the customer experience in daily decision-making and empowering the middle and frontline employees to make decisions that transform the customer experience in their daily roles. While leadership at the top determines the course of the business and steers it along the path, your middle management and frontline employees have the real power to transform the culture.

Yes, customer service training is good to develop your team's skills but here are four steps that constantly keep the focus on the customer and are easily integrated into daily activities without tasking your team with additional projects.

Idea #1: Incorporate these three questions in your weekly meetings and conversations

Question 1: "How would I want to be treated if I were the customer?"

Don't be fooled by the simplicity of this question. It immediately focuses the attention on why we do what we do and prevents tunnel vision. I have found that when teams ask this question of themselves, they come up with better solutions to problems. During weekly sales meetings, the focus shifts to adding value to the customer instead of pushing and nagging for an appointment or a sale.

Moreover, it's also a great way to keep the office politics and individual agendas at bay and improve collaboration. In one of the companies I consult with, there was a constant struggle between the legal department and the sales team. Each of them had KPIs to meet, so it was only natural that they would focus on getting that done. But approaching your colleague with, "I need you to get this approved so I can meet my sales goal," is not exactly productive.

During one of our coaching sessions, I had the sales director approach the legal department with a slightly different question: "What is the best solution for this [insert problem] and how would it make me feel if I were the customer?" By shifting the focus to the customer, it is no longer a question of me vs. you, but rather of what's important to the customer.

Immediately the legal team started coming up with different solutions that they ran past the customer question criterion till they arrived at something that would logically make sense for everyone.

Question 2: "What did our customers love about us?"

By asking this you consciously acknowledge the positive work you and your teams are doing. This will keep you motivated to continue doing more of this good work.

Question 3: What could we have done differently to add value to the customer?

This is a great question as it prompts you to analyze why sales are stuck in the pipeline or why you didn't close a contract. It can help you to better understand how to deliver on your promise to the customer.

Idea #2: Ensure everyone can see/understand how the customer moves through the buying process

One of the tools that my clients find very useful is a visual process map that shows how the customer moves through the entire buying process, not just the sales process. Not only does this create an understanding of how each department relies on one another to serve the customer but keeps out the silo mentality.

Each department has this process map on their wall with this question written at the top.

How do we make their journey memorable when they pass through our department?

Having a visual reminder such as this keeps the main purpose in focus and brings meaning to mundane activities that need to be done.

Idea #3: Incorporate the "huddle" approach to solve problems quickly each day rather than holding weekly meetings that everyone dreads

The huddle approach is outlined by Verne Harnish in his book, *Mastering the Rockefeller Habits.*[29] Here's how a huddle can create urgency and set the tempo for performance. Representatives from each department get together for a quick meeting every day. Nobody is allowed to sit because the idea is to get to the issue right away and solve it. Everyone is asked three questions as we go around the room:

1. What are you working on?

2. What's the bottleneck?

3. What can be done to resolve it?

---

29   Harnish, V (2007) *Mastering the Rockefeller Habits*. New Delhi: Dreamtech Press.

The huddle is a great way to get everyone up to speed with what is going on, what everyone is working on and the progress of the project. Also, bottlenecks are identified and anticipated asap and can be resolved immediately too. Nobody is allowed to go into an in-depth discussion. If more information and details are needed, the concerned parties get together outside of the huddle and solve it.

You may wonder why we need this in a world of email, project plans and WhatsApp. That's exactly why we need this. Because of this information over-load, we all suffer from tunnel vision and sometimes can't see beyond the obvious.

Moreover, a huddle reduces the need for constant meetings which in essence are more about damage control and reporting than active brainstorming. Teams are working together better because problems are solved even before they arise.

Idea #4: Harness the power of the "wow metric" in reporting

Appreciating and recognizing your teams/departments goes a long way in cementing the importance of customer experience. It also starts at the top. Recently, I was traveling to Nigeria and was concerned about security and transport arrangements from the airport to the hotel as it was my first time there. My travel agent in Kenya assured me that he would take care of everything and that I had no reason to worry. Sure enough, there was someone to pick me up when I arrived. Unfortunately, my phone died so he had no way to contact me directly and find out if I had arrived. He went the extra mile to contact the hotel and tracked down the driver who was picking me up to make sure that I was OK, doing all this from across the continent in Kenya.

I was so touched and impressed by the customer service that I wrote to his manager to acknowledge the great service. A week later, I received a personal email from the CEO himself on how much he appreciated me taking time to write about this employee and thanked me for it. He didn't have to do it. It was pretty evident that the culture of customer satisfaction started at the top.

Here's a fun metric that some of my clients have started using to keep the customer at the forefront. It's called the "wow metric." Besides sales, financial, and operations data, every month each department has to share at least one "wow" moment they created for their customer (could be internal or external). The department with the most creative and highest number of wows, wins and gets publicly recognized at the company meeting and internal communications. It keeps a healthy competition going between all departments and empowers individuals to make decisions that create more win-win situations for everyone.

CEO Thomas Watson Jr. of IBM is credited with building the most highly trained sales team in the world. The IBM sales team was the envy of many competitors for almost thirty years. What enabled them to succeed continuously was how the entire organizational structure was designed to serve the customer to the best of their ability. The sales team had the backing, knowledge, and expertise of the entire organization so that they were able to add value and serve the customer to the best of their ability. It is vital that sales leaders, operations experts, financial gurus and everyone else in the organization understand that the customer is the center of the process.

When your customers are looked after, they become your sales force in turn. In the next chapter we'll look at some ways of training your customers to become your best sales force. They'll only do that if you've trained your sales team to take care of them!

Chapter summary

1. Create a perfect vision of the sales process, centered on the prospect, and ensure this vision is understood by everyone in the sales team.

2. Integrate the four steps to build customer experience into your sales process.

3. The sales experience is as important as your product because your prospect doesn't just buy your

product or service but also the experience of doing business with you.

4. The sales process is just a part of the customer experience. Facilitate cross-functional and interdepartmental sessions so that everyone learns about the customer's needs.

5. Look at your sales process in the context of the whole delivery cycle and involve both marketing and operations in problem-solving.

6. Select any of the four ideas to become customer-centric in your product delivery cycle.

10
Never Underestimate The Power Of Referrals

"Our referral program is great but I don't believe our sales teams are taking advantage of it to close sales," said Martin, country director of a technology company I work with. My experience has been that, behind statements like these, there is often more to the story than may at first be evident. I asked Victor, the head of sales, if he thought his teams were maximizing the opportunities from the referral program.

"We are using that as a sales tool," he said. "But operations haven't done a great job of keeping their promise when it comes to meeting timelines for delivery. For instance, last month we were supposed to deliver the project to clients, but the project ran into delays and we still haven't finished and delivered on time. It puts our sales team in a difficult spot, and I believe that is affecting their referrals."

An incentive program is a good start, but it is only a piece of the larger puzzle of the referral system that works. Successful businesses and salespeople that attribute **50% of their business to referrals or repeat business** follow a slightly different model to attract clients. They realize that acceptance and trust within a person's circle of influence are far stronger motivators than a referral fee. First, they focus on investing in their existing clients and creating an experience that strengthens their relationships with these clients instead of relying primarily on the monetary incentive.

The focus on relationships creates a valuable and loyal client database and leverages their clients to bring in new customers who are already pre-sold on their value.

So how do you go about putting in place a referral system that works? That's where the Client Sale Force Pyramid comes in.

Why did you stop visiting a business you regularly visited? Unless you moved or it was no longer convenient my guess is, the underlying feeling was probably one of perceived indifference from the business. It was easy to switch loyalty because the message you probably got was, "We don't really care about you."

It's easy to fall into the trap and assume that if a customer has bought from you they will come back to you whenever they have a need. Nothing can be further from the truth. In reality, satisfied customers are not loyal customers.

Satisfied customers are just parked on your doorstep and will gladly move along when they find a better deal. Proper advertising, product promotion, and market share pricing are all important, but at the end of the day, goods aren't sold; products and services are bought. As Daniel Pink says in his book, *To Sell is Human*, "We live in an age when *caveat emptor*, or 'buyer beware,' has been replaced with *caveat venditor*, or 'seller beware.' When sellers are no longer the 'purveyors of information' and everyone has access to information, the scale tilts in the favor of the customer."[30]

The Client Sales Force Pyramid

The Client Sales Force Pyramid looks at the buying psychology of your potential clients, the various types of clients in your business, and how to turn these clients into your Sales Force. Let's take a look at the Client Sales Force Pyramid, from bottom to top.

---

30   Pink, DH (2018) *To Sell Is Human: The Surprising Truth About Persuading, Convincing, and Influencing Others.* Edinburgh: Canongate Books.

The Client Sales Force Pyramid

Your Target Market

Everyone out there that may or may not have a need for your service. You just want to reach them through marketing because you think they could use your services.

Prospects

They have a need for your service, have heard about you, and are interested in initiating a conversation with you.

One-time Buyers

They are ready to give you a try but there is a good probability they will move somewhere else if they get a better deal. They are parked in the 10-minute parking spot. They might purchase once because they received a great deal but there is no guarantee they'll return. There's also the possibility that they are simply hopping from one business to another for the attractive deals.

Customers

They've bought from you a couple of times and are probably in your database. There is a small level of trust but the moment you mess up they will be gone. Beware, don't mistake these satisfied customers for loyal customers.

Promoters

They buy from you regularly. It has become a habit: you've won their trust and they keep coming back. Your Promoters feel like they belong in your business. Think of the places you visit often. You probably have a grocery store or a restaurant that you frequently end up at. They will be happy to refer you when someone has a need for your services and asks them for a recommendation.

Client Sales Force

They believe in you, value your relationship, and want to share your gift with the rest of the word because it makes them look like a hero. They will talk about how great you are and SELL you without waiting for someone to ask them. I am part of my daughter's school's Client Sales Force because I absolutely believe in them. The school never has to ask me to sell them. I do it on my own accord. I even send out emails to my friends saying, "If you are looking for a great school you should check out KRK…" and I ramble on about why they are so great.

How to avoid the number 1 mistake every business makes (and that you're probably making now)

With traditional marketing campaigns, the focus is on turning your target market into prospects. A whole lot of time and money goes into getting someone interested enough in the business to pick up the phone and ask a question. The sales rep does a great job at the sales presentation and comes back with a check. There's a big sigh of relief, as it gets them closer to their sales target for the month, and the new client is transferred to the email marketing list for customers. The sales rep makes a mental note to keep in touch with the client regularly.

For the most part, the rep's job is done and they can sit back and relax because the customer will come back when they need your services again. It's now time to move on to the next client. And so the cycle to get new customers starts over again with brand new, savvy campaigns to transition people in the Target Market category to the One-time Buyer level, or even to the Customer level, and then stop right there.

Then comes the day when the rep really needs to meet their monthly quota and the One-time Buyer client comes to mind. A pang of guilt reminds them that they should have kept in touch with the client more frequently like they had intended. But life got in the way.

"It couldn't be that bad," the sales rep reasons. "They've probably been getting emails from us. I should just call and ask for a referral. I can tell them about the incentive program."

Most businesses spend *six times as much* trying to turn the Target Market into Prospects or One-time Buyers than they do trying to turn these One-time Buyers into their Client Sales Force.

A good majority of clients within a company's database sit in the One-time Buyers or Customer category indefinitely. All the sales team's efforts are focused on getting new clients to these two levels when your existing clients have the potential to go all the way and become your Sales Force! Why would you stop focusing and investing in them when they get to the Customer level?

It's much easier to sell to someone who already trusts you than someone you have never seen before.

Think of it this way. What would the impact on your business be if you could turn just 20% of your customers into your Sales Force?

The Client Sales Force Model means that you should focus your marketing efforts and budget not just on new lead-generation efforts but on creating an experience that moves your Prospects and One-time Buyers up the pyramid. The One-time Buyers graduate to becoming your Client Sales Force who promote your business and send you new Prospects, thereby keeping your pipeline consistently full.

Moving Prospects to the top of the Client Sales Force Pyramid

When you focus your efforts on taking your prospects to the top of the pyramid and turning them into your Client Sales Force:

- You don't have to worry about repeat business

- Your clients will stay longer

- Your clients will do the selling for you

- You'll create a steady stream of qualified leads that don't have to be SOLD

- You'll be spending more time with people you enjoy working with

  Client Sales Force = more referrals + more money + more time + more happiness

Eleven strategies to get your clients to sell for you

So how can you use the Client Sales Force Model in your business to get referrals and repeat clients? Most businesses already have pieces of the Client Sales Force Model in place, so they have a goldmine that they are sitting on, but it is not producing the results that they want.

Take the following steps to systematize your process for strategically and proactively getting referrals.

Strategy #1: Know your numbers

Just like you would with any marketing campaign, ask yourself: "What's the goal of our referral program?" How would you measure the success of your referral program?

Measurement drives behavior. Simply measuring something can stimulate improvement, even without a huge change in the activity required. By having a goal and measuring success against it, you will be able to tell if you are maximizing the referrals you could be getting—or if your team is leaving money on the table.

Secondly ask, "What percentage of our marketing budget is allocated toward existing clients?" (You might want to think about this question again once you have finished reading this chapter.)

Strategy#2: Build these two crucial elements into your service

A few months ago, I was visiting my mother-in-law in Toronto and she suggested a Chinese restaurant known for its great food. I made reservations for eight people at 7pm so we could go to a movie later. We arrived at the restaurant only to find that there were no tables available and we would have to wait. "But we have a reservation," I told the owner.

He looked at me unapologetically. His look said, "There's nothing I can do about it. You'll just have to wait."

Forty-five minutes later, we had a table and had placed our orders. When the food arrived, it was great, but by this time, we were put off because we had missed our movie. When I called my friend the next day, what do you think I told her? "Yeah, the food was good, but we had to wait for forty-five minutes and we missed our movie!"

As far as the restaurant was concerned, they delivered great food, and I should have been happy. But as a customer, I didn't go there for great food alone. I was also expecting a good dining experience.

Your client buys two things from you:

1. Your service
2. The emotional experience of doing business with you

It's easy to fall into the trap of focusing primarily on delivering your service versus the client's overall experience. We discussed this in the previous chapter.

Why care about the emotional experience? We all have an innate need to feel important and cared for. Customers will forgive incompetence if you make it right, but they will not forgive a lack of interest or perceived indifference.

Make the overall experience of doing business with you memorable. Don't deliver your service without an extraordinary experience.

Strategy #3: Design an emotional experience

Step into the shoes of your customer for a few minutes and picture exactly how you would like YOUR business to treat YOU. What do you want to feel when you call or walk in? How would you like to be greeted? What experience do you want to leave with? Feel free to borrow ideas from other businesses.

Think of your favorite store or a business that you go to all the time. What do they do to make you feel special? Start creating a vision of perfection centered on the customer that involves not just the result the client expects to get but also the experience they would like to have.

Creating special moments does not have to be expensive. It just takes caring enough to actually do it!

Emotion trumps logic

People often intuitively reach a buying decision based upon their emotional response and then back it up with a logical reason. If, during the first meeting with your prospect, the emotional experience is lacking, the likelihood that they will buy is slim. If they happen to buy, chances are they will stop at the One-time Buyer or Customer level and not progress to becoming your Client Sales Force.

Strategy #4: Get your team on board

Baptist Healthcare System is an organization that understands how to transform customer experience from mediocre to extraordinary. How do they do that? By understanding and applying the power of behavioral vision. That means identifying and clearly defining what behaviors and actions constitute a great experience and having employees act upon that.

For instance, if a patient asks a staff member for directions, the staff member is expected to take them there versus giving them directions. A higher priority is placed on helping patients and customers than getting on with the task at hand. Talk about a positive emotional experience!

Define your vision

Your team plays a crucial role in the experience your prospects and clients receive. Define your vision of how you want clients treated. Interpret expectations into behaviors and actions for team members to execute. This is not just a customer service exercise, by the way. It permeates the whole organization, whether it is sales, accounts, operations, or any other department.

Part of defining your vision is accepting input from all possible sources. I imagine you already have a process for delivery of your service. A great strategy is to ask your team members directly what could be improved or changed. You will be surprised at what you find out from them.

Strategy #5: Remove the irritants

As you translate your vision of the ideal client experience into your processes, you'll notice bumps along the way. There is no better way to find out what bothers your clients than to ask them. You cannot create this vision in isolation of what your customer wants.

Survey your customers

I know this is a scary thought. You are certainly putting yourself on the spot. After all, what if you don't like what you hear? But the only way you can fix things is to find out what's wrong.

This is one instance where I can safely say that "silence is not golden." There is often a hidden message in that silence, and it is not a good one.

Go on the journey

There is nothing like experiencing your business first-hand—walking a mile in your customer's shoes. That's right. I am talking about mystery shopping, which is perhaps the one thing that makes sales teams shudder more than customer surveys.

Nothing else will give you a more accurate analysis of what's really going on. What we experience is engraved in our minds, and most times, a mystery shopping experience is a far better way of spurring action than a fancy customer service analytics report designed for the boardroom meeting.

Strategy #6: Consistently deliver high-quality service and a positive experience

Now that you have your vision pinned down and have fixed the irritants along the way, what next? Now, it's time to deliver consistently!

Consistency creates credibility and trust. Nobody understands that better than McDonald's. No matter where you are in the world, if you walk into a McDonald's, you know exactly what to expect.

With any new relationship, people are wary of being burned. They tread cautiously. Prospects and One-time Buyers can only move up the pyramid when you win their trust. So how do you become as consistent and reliable as McDonald's? **Consistency comes with having a system in place.** Systems allow you to guarantee delivery and a minimum standard of performance consistently. Systematize not just the process of delivery of your product or service but more importantly, the experience.

Strategy #7: Find and invest in your untapped Client Sales Force

Just as you have a profile of your ideal customer or a buyer persona that you target in your marketing campaigns, it is important to distinguish the clients in your database that have the potential of becoming your Client Sales Force or referral givers. Think about your top five clients. Now, answer the following:

- Why do you enjoy working with them?

- What are some of the traits you associate with these five clients?

- What do they value the most about working with you? Is it quality, price, customer service, reliability, speed, image, convenience?

- Is there a common theme in your top five clients? Perhaps an industry sector that you clearly prefer to work with?

Not all clients are created equal. In most businesses, clients are likely to fall into one of four categories:

1. **Amazing:** They perfectly fit the profile of your dream or ideal client.

2. **Bread winners:** They are the core of your business.

3. **Complainers:** They are always whining about something, but you appreciate their business.

4. **Dread them:** You can't stand them, but they keep coming back.

What category do most of your clients fall under? The purpose of categorizing your clients is to determine who you will want to focus on and move up the pyramid to become part of your Client Sales Force. Clearly, A and B clients have the potential to move up and become your Client Sales Force when you invest in them. But hold on a minute...

Consider your C and D clients. How do you feel working with them? What do they make you do for them? Discount your prices? Over-service them? Go the extra mile to make them happy or just to get their jobs done faster because you can't stand to hear them complain one more time? Incidentally, how many referrals have they brought in, and how much money are you actually making from them?

What happens to your A clients?

My guess is that you really enjoy working with your A clients. They are probably worth a lot in real dollars to your business. They don't complain or waste your time. They are easy to work with, they are low maintenance, and it doesn't take much to keep them happy.

Then the C and D clients come along and ruin everything.

It's easy to divert your attention away from your A clients to fix the recurring complaints of C and D clients—people who will never be happy. The "squeaky wheel gets the grease." Or, in this case, the person who complains the loudest is heard. And while your attention is focused on your C and D clients, your A and B clients are not feeling valued.

Statistics show that 63% of customers leave businesses because they don't feel they are important enough or treated in a special way. Before you neglect an A client to put out the fires being started by C and D clients, ask yourself, "What will be the impact on my business if an A client starts feeling that they aren't valued enough and decides to leave?" I imagine the consequences will be much worse than if a C or D client decides to move on.

Strategy #8: Wow your Client Sales Force

Delivering great results and a great experience will keep your database loyal for the most part and bring referrals. However, if you want to bring in new customers, being competent is not good enough.

There has to be something interesting and remarkable about what you do and how you do it that makes your clients say, "Wow, that was a great experience! How did they do that? I've got to tell my friends." You don't have to run a paragliding school to come up with your interesting story.

We all love to share something out of the ordinary with people around us. Think of what you want your clients saying about you to their friends. The best part is, **every business can do this.**

Let's say you own a plumbing company, and you do a great job. You will get business thanks to the quality of your work, of course. But is it very unlikely that your customer will tell a friend at a dinner party, "I called the plumber, and he fixed the toilet. It doesn't leak anymore"? Even though that's exactly what they hired you to do, merely doing your job wouldn't be enough to garner a glowing review. If, however, you showed up with your toolbox in a dinner suit with a red carnation, you can bet you'll come up in con-versation. "Guess what happened when I called this plumbing company? The guy showed up in a suit!" OK, so that may be a slightly farfetched example, but you get the point, right?

What's your story?

If you depend on word of mouth marketing for your business and referrals, you need to inspire a really great story they just have to tell. You need to arm your Client Sales Force with a story that they can tell people who have never heard about you.

This boils down to one simple concept: Your prospects have to hear about you before they get the chance to experience your skill and ability at what you do. Stories allow people to connect on an emotional level with you. So, what is your story?

Strategy #9: Systematize the five must-dos for easy referrals

When you focus on providing great results, a great experience, and a great story to tell, you will get referrals. A word of caution! Don't stop here if you want to make this a consistent predictable strategy for generating new and repeat business.

You have to ask for referrals. But how and when should you ask for referrals in a way that is comfortable? Here are five things that you can share with your sales team that will allow them to ask for referrals easily, consistently and in a way that builds relationships.

1. Position your clients early to give you referrals, preferably at the beginning of the relationship. It can be difficult to ask for referrals if you haven't set up the expectation correctly.

2. Stay in touch with clients. A regular timeline of communication is essential for keeping you connected to them. When you are constantly in touch with your clients and past clients, it is much easier to ask for referrals than it is to make an unexpected call, six months down the road, that says, "Remember me? I'm looking for referrals."

3. Know when to ask for referrals. I was at a doctor's office the other day and saw a sign that said, "Please tell your friends and family about us." I mean it's a good reminder, but I can quite honestly say I have never given anyone a referral from a sign like this. Think about it. The business has not done anything to build a relationship with me yet; it's like putting the cart before the horse. There is a time and a way to ask for referrals. You want to ask clients for referrals when you have delivered on their expectations and they feel good about you. If you haven't built the relationship or delivered on the results, don't ask for referrals. Take a look at your process. Where can you build in the opportunity to get a referral?

4. Educate your clients on how to give you referrals. Often times, we assume that our clients can read our minds and know the type of referrals we want and when we want them. Don't do that. Tell them exactly what you are looking for and the best way for them to give you a referral. Always ask in a manner that is genuine.

5. Make it easy for your clients to give you referrals. The less work they have to do, the easier it is for them to give referrals. Have a system in place that offers suggestions and walks them through the process step by step.

Strategy #10: Reward your Client Sales Force consistently

If you focus on building a transformational experience for your clients and reward them for being great clients, you automatically create the incentive for them to give you referrals. Your referral program will have more power when you have done the above because your clients have confidence in your service and experience and giving you a referral makes them look good to their peers. While a financial incentive may be important, it is not the only driver for referrals. Our need as human beings for acceptance is far greater.

A referral is a gift, so don't take it for granted. Regardless of whether or not you close the sale, thank the person who gave you the referral. Show appreciation for their efforts.

Strategy #11: Prioritize transformation over transaction

When you are focused on just delivering your service well without building an emotional contract with your client, your relationship can best be described as transactional. Transactional relationships can be easily replaced. But when you choose to build a relationship and create an emotional experience for your clients and team, your relationship becomes transformational, and your clients will turn into your sales force.

Nelson Boswell sums it up best. "Here is a simple but powerful rule—always give people more than what they expect to get."

Chapter summary

1. An incentive program is a good start, but it is only a piece of the larger puzzle of a referral system that works. Acceptance and trust within a person's circle of influence are far stronger motivators than a referral fee.

2. Satisfied customers are not necessarily loyal customers.

3. Understanding how the Client Sales Force Model works focuses your marketing efforts and budget not just on new lead-generation efforts but on creating an experience that transforms your One-time Buyers into your biggest advocates.

4. When your sales team is focused on the customer, their service/product needs and their emotional experience needs, you can create a Customer Sales Force that drives referrals to your business.

5. Not all clients are created equal. Focus your attention on the most promising people and invest in them to become your Client Sales Force.

6. Use the eleven strategies to proactively and systematically increase your referrals and get more repeat business.

FACTOR FOUR
SALES COACHING—COACH FOR BUSINESS IMPACT

11
How To Create A Culture Of Coaching For Performance

Imagine an Olympic athlete training without a coach. Or a graduate-level course of study without any professors. Sounds preposterous, doesn't it?

Winning the Olympics takes more than just the athlete practicing and training rigorously. A fairly elaborate support structure goes hand in hand to boost performance. At the US Olympic Training Center in Chula Vista, California, an entire team of nutritionists, exercise physiologists, sports medicine specialists and coaches work with athletes to help them meet their targets as they discuss their strengths and weaknesses and adjust their diets and recovery techniques for peak performance. The same goes for becoming an authority in a field of academic study. Nobody reaches that level without educational training and guidance.

Principals of leading companies understand that sales success doesn't just depend on the sales rep sticking to his or her performance routines. Maximizing performance is about having a structure in place that enables peak performance. Simply put, coaching for performance is a must-have at all levels of the organization!

So, why exactly does coaching work so well? As John Whitmore, author of *Coaching for Performance*, says, "Coaching is unlocking a person's potential to maximize their own performance. It is helping them to learn rather than teaching them."[31]

Adults learn by doing, and coaching is about helping people gather their own insights and lessons from their experience to help them make the behavioral change needed to be more effective. As a sales manager it is tempting to tell a salesperson they need to make more calls, but what is more effective is asking the salesperson what they think is the best way for them to get more leads. They might come up with a solution that you probably never even thought of.

Coaching vs. commanding

Coaching is a key tool in your sales manager's toolkit that can maximize the effectiveness of each

---

31 Whitmore, J (2017) *Coaching for Performance: The Principles and Practice of Coaching and Leadership (updated 25th anniversary edition)*. London: Nicholas Brealey.

individual team member. Instead of demanding and controlling results, managers are more effective when they develop a partnership with their team built on a shared understanding of what goals need to be accomplished and how they will be accomplished.

How can coaching help your manager meet their quotas?

When numbers are down, the default style of steering performance resembles this: "Our numbers are down, we need to catch up this quarter and I want everybody to ramp up their activity. I want to see more calls and more appointments if we are to hit our targets."

When you tell your already overworked team they need to work harder to get to their goal, the results are counterproductive. They have heard your lecture before, they will probably put in that extra effort for a bit but it is not a strategy that will sustain performance long-term.

From a scientific perspective, why doesn't the command approach work? A command to get results often triggers and activates the fight or flight mode in our brains. While we are more alert when dealing with a negative situation in the moment, and prepared for attack under stress, operating in the fight or flight mode bypasses our rational mind which is responsible for logic, creativity, and problem-solving. It reduces our cognitive ability and creative intellectual capacity.

Our ability to distinguish relevant information better, absorb new information quicker and think more strategically is reduced and negatively impacts performance by 20–30%.

Contrast this with a coaching approach that focuses on problem-solving. "Our numbers are down. We have a 20% gap to close. What do we need to do to get three more deals this month?" Not only does this engage your team in problem-solving and stimulates thinking, but it actively taps into your team's resourcefulness to get results.

Get your managers to work with a coach who can give them feedback on how they interact with their team members. Well worth the investment to upskill them. Trying to transform your team without having coaching in place is a waste of time and resources. The more you invest in building that skill set the better it is translated into your team's results.

What can coaching do for sales reps?

Among other things, coaching can help sales reps close new accounts more quickly, develop long-term skills that will propel their sales career, and over-come obstacles that hold them back from maximizing performance.

Coaching a sales rep could involve working on a cold call script, learning how to handle an objection, or confronting their own beliefs and fears around rejections. Sales coaches help reps set goals and strategies focused on maximizing impact and time to reach targets. They can provide feedback and guidance to help sales reps change the behaviors that impede performance. By developing new habits and behaviors, reps can execute action plans to reach their targets.

Who should coach?

Companies where sales managers play a significant part in coaching see significant improvement in results. With one of our clients, the manager's compensation is tied to the amount invested in coaching. Managers meet with their reps once a week to look at progress on goals, strategies and how plans are executed. Coaching often involves managers working with reps to prepare them for a big call, role-playing potential questions, objections, and a debrief call afterwards.

Managers also give direct and immediate advice if needed or ask self-exploratory questions that get the rep to reflect on behaviors and skills they applied, and the results. They have them focus on how a "strength" can be incorporated in future scenarios or change a behavior that may not have worked.

The ability to reach out and brainstorm with their coach gives the reps the focus and solutions they need to move forward in their goals and reduces the learning curve. Whether you train your managers to become great sales coaches or hire external coaches, getting to the next level of performance requires coaching.

Coaching to deal with performance issues

The primary goal of a performance evaluation is to develop the strengths of an individual to enable them to contribute effectively through their role to the organization's goal. It is also about identifying the areas in which employees may need support or improvement to meet their objectives. Evaluating performance against goals is meaningful and purposeful when the primary focus is on removing the obstacles that get in the way of performance instead of focusing simply on the problem. Unfortunately, that is the trap most companies find themselves in when it comes to performance evaluation. With an inordinate amount of emphasis being on evaluation versus development, the effectiveness of the exercise is reduced.

HR practice leader for the research firm CEB, Brian Kropp shares how companies like Google, GE, Cargill, Accenture, Eli Lilly, Adobe, and others are changing their approach to performance management. The primary focus for these companies instead is on developing the skills of individuals and frequent feedback to employees.

For instance, at Cargill managers incorporate daily encouragement and feedback into conversations with their teams. Constructive feedback that doesn't dwell on past mistakes—but instead focuses on these as "lessons" and opportunities for developments in future situations—have led to measurable improvements in employee motivation and engagement. This is particularly significant when it comes to managing a sales team for performance.

In a technology company that I coach, sales managers are trained in coaching skills that enable them to handle difficult conversations and give immediate feedback on performance with a plan for action. Managing sales behavior is far more effective than simply looking at sales results. While sales results are important it is a historical snapshot in time.

For example, if your rep did not meet their goal of adding three new accounts, there is not much that is going to come out of the conversation by focusing on why the goals weren't met. Instead, the conversation is going to be more productive if you work through the goals, expected results, and the behaviors needed to meet those goals. For instance, in that conversation, as you agree on expectations and goals you expect, also emphasize key behaviors you would like to observe and monitor.

If bringing in three new accounts is the expected result, the daily behavior you want to see may include how the rep prepares his or her plan to meet key decision makers, the number of appointments booked per day, or how they might be bringing new opportunities to the table. By observing behavior on a frequent basis, coaches intervene and can provide immediate guidance that can affect results. During one such conversation, when the weekly appointments were not being met, the manager immediately addressed the issue with the sales rep and helped bring him on track. Had he waited for the whole month, it would have been too late, and the rep would surely have missed his targets.

Being able to coach your sales team to maximize performance means that managers have to understand what motivates their team members, and how to incorporate it in day-to-day activities.

Understanding motivation and reward systems

"I don't think the sales team feels appreciated by the rest of the organization," said Linda, a head of sales who manages a high-performance team of eight individuals. "The perception people have is that the sales team is highly paid for not doing all that much work. They're always out on client lunches and meeting people. That's not so hard, right? Of course, the people who think that have no idea how tough the market has been with the economy. To beat our goals despite that has been a lot of hard work. Last week during our company meeting, I made it a point to recognize my team in front of everyone. They deserved that and needed that."

Over the past twelve months, Linda's team had been consistently beating their monthly targets. In fact, her team had met their yearly quota for one of their product lines by the third quarter and still had a whole quarter to go. A key reason her team succeeded and surpassed their targets was Linda's belief and understanding that peak performance requires more than monetary compensation. Motivation is a key determinant of high performance.

So, where does motivation come from, and how do we systematically build it? Is it more money? More rewards? A good pep talk? What works?

Often, when companies are trying to create reward programs the question that gets asked is, "Should we do team-building days for our sales team to motivate them or shall we have contests, or do we need to give them more monetary incentives? What will work better?" Without an understanding of how our needs as human beings are met, designing reward systems and trying to motivate our teams is a little like putting the cart before the horse.

Keep in mind that what works for one organization may not work for you because you have two completely different cultures. Without an understanding of your culture, sales motivation programs become an exercise in trial and error and may not achieve your desired results.

Maslow's hierarchy of needs and how they relate to sales

How you motivate people begins with an understanding of how to use Maslow's hierarchy of needs. According to Maslow,[32] we are motivated by five basic needs:

1. **Physiological (or the basic need to survive):** In the context of sales, this would include a basic salary/commission/compensation structure.

2. **Safety and security:** We need to feel safe, whether that means physically or economically. Interpreted in sales terms, tools to get the job done and a work environment where it is safe to share ideas and challenge assumptions.

3. **Social/sense of belonging:** This is the need to be part of a group, to have the ability to connect, to share, and to inspire each other.

4. **Self-esteem:** This isn't just about feeling good about yourself. It's about the need to feel respected and to work with a sense of self-confidence. In a sales context, this means a salesperson being recognized for an achievement

---

32 McLeod, S (2018) "Maslow's Hierarchy of Needs." www.simplypsychology.org/maslow.html

or singled out for the importance of their contribution to the organization.

5. **Self-actualization:** This is the desire for self-fulfillment and developing to one's full potential. In other words, it means feeling empowered to develop and grow and move to the next level in their careers.

According to Maslow's theory, lower-level needs have to be satisfied or met first before people will try to move to the next level and eventually reach their full potential. In other words, basic physiological needs are prioritized over safety needs, which are prioritized over social needs, and so on.

How does this all relate to motivation for your sales teams? Well, if your sales team are not where they need to be financially, a monetary compensation might be the right motivator for performance because it might help them meet their basic physiological needs.

Your sales reps also need to feel secure about their jobs (safety and security needs) and be in an environment that allows them to express themselves in order for them to move up the pyramid and develop to their full potential.

The fear of lay-offs and job insecurity might make them work harder but will not allow them to fulfill the other needs they have and develop as a result. They could continue in this environment for some time but eventually burn out or look for another company. At this stage, more money may cease to be a motivating factor; a better motivator is to create a work environment that provides sales reps with tools to reach their goals, and allows them to share their ideas and receive concerns or feedback from clients without fear of repercussions.

Similarly, high performers might choose to follow their managers to a new company if they have a great relationship with them and not necessarily need a huge pay rise to make that decision. We have an innate desire to grow as people and that doesn't stem from a lack of something but rather the ability to fulfill our growth needs.

Barry is one of the top sales performers of a company I train. One day, he came up to me after our session and confided in me, "I got an offer from this company and they are giving me a higher salary."

"So, are you looking to move then?" I asked.

"Well, it is attractive, but I have a great team here," said Barry. "I have worked hard to get to my position in this company and I am being considered as the lead sales rep for the new product we are launching. I am excited about that and have grown so much as a person. At the end of the day, I think I could make that money easily. I am thinking it's not the right time to move."

When your self-esteem needs are being met like Barry's, career growth might be a better motivator.

Effective reward systems that meet the five basic needs

As you think of how to motivate your team, ask this question first: "What needs are not being met right now?" That will help you determine if a contest, reward or commission increase is the right motivator.

Here is a quick checklist and questions that can help determine what motivators would be important for your team.

Type of need	Questions to consider	Examples of motivators
Physiological	How does my salary and commission structure compare with the market? Will it allow my sales team to focus on building long-term relationships with clients or tempt them to make deals just to earn the commission?	• Pay • Commission structures • Reimbursements for fuel, client lunches, networking events etc
Safety and security	Does my sales team have tools and skills to help them generate new leads, get meetings? Is our company image helping them sell or making it hard for them to sell? Do they feel safe to share the insights they are getting from the market about our products?	• Marketing support for creation of tools • PR campaigns/events to positively affect company image • Training in skills • An environment where ideas are encouraged and listened to objectively

Continued

Type of need	Questions to consider	Examples of motivators
Social/sense of belonging	Can the team rely on each other to help them out?	• Team outings and team-building days • Social activities • Tag-teaming with each other on sales calls • Sales meetings that focus on brainstorming and problem-solving
Self-esteem	Are they recognized?	• Company recognition programs • Contests • Best performer awards • Coaching to work on self-confidence and self-esteem
Self-actualization	What would be the next level of growth?	• Career development plans • Coaching to unleash staff potential

Most behaviors can be motivated by more than one basic need. For instance, when someone is looking for a promotion all three needs may be at play, the need for a higher salary (physiological need), a better title (self-esteem), and the ability to do what they love most (self-actualization). Understanding the basis of how Maslow's needs work can help leaders create an environment that will keep their teams motivated and also identify how to deal with motivational issues.

Below are a few common options for types of rewards.

Monetary compensation

Money might work as a short-term boost to perfor-mance but will not necessarily deliver long-term growth. As the basic physiological need for money and security is satisfied it stops becoming a motivator and people crave more than money to perform.

Building safety

Janice is a top performer on a sales team I coach. However, when it comes to speaking up and ex-pressing her views she visibly shies away from that. Because I have the privilege of knowing and coaching her top boss, Jim, I know that he values differences of opinions and is not necessarily looking for everyone to agree. Somehow, along the way, this is not the per-ception that his sales team has developed of him.

The team has some great ideas that he needs to know about, but they hesitate to share them. One of the things we started in monthly sales meetings with Jim was to nominate someone from the sales team to play the role of devil's advocate and look for what could go wrong in implementing a new sales idea. Any oppos-ing views were presented respectfully by the devil's advocate to the group and usually began with the phrase, "Have we considered what will happen if...?"

Because the expectation of the role requires you to come up with ideas that actively encourage contradiction in a safe and non-threatening way, it encourages people to express themselves and actively listen to each other's opinions. This is just one of many ways to build safety within the group.

Incorporating recognition

Speaker slots are a great option in this area. A company that I worked with had an annual sales conference where top performers were invited to share their lessons for success and areas of expertise with the rest of the team.

Taking on the role of guest speaker carries a certain level of prestige. Not only did this give top performers a bit of visibility and authority, but it also gave them purpose as being part of something bigger and being able to influence the lives of their peers by being seen as mentors.

Awards

Another company regularly recognizes top performers at quarterly company-wide meetings by thanking them for their contribution publicly and showing the impact they have had on the progress of the company. When quarterly targets are achieved, they might even get a personal thank you note or call from the CEO.

One real estate company changed the title of its sales reps from "sales executives" to "real estate investment advisors." This title positioned them as experts and advisors, which changed the way they viewed their role with their clients. It increased their overall self-esteem, and they felt more ownership of the project. After all, no one was better positioned to advise clients on properties than them. It also fulfilled their need for being respected by peers and professionals alike.

A company in Atlanta regularly reserves box tickets at shows and sporting events for top performers where they get to interact with senior executives and get visibility. Not only is that a great motivation for sales professionals for whom career growth is important but it also gives them a perspective of the greater purpose of the company and how they fit in. Another company organizes a beach get-away if the team hits their results, which is a great way to foster team performance and camaraderie.

Career growth

Discussions of career growth are often neglected during the year and left for annual performance reviews. This is a powerful, yet under-employed, source of motivation. If an employee expresses their interest in a leadership position, a great motivator for the person would be access to training in the skills needed to be a manager. People have to keep progressing up the hierarchy of needs to grow.

More importantly, leaders that understand how motivation works focus on incorporating it in a daily environment; they understand that while rewards and recognition are important, if the daily work environment does not change to allow people to share ideas freely and have tools to work, long-term performance is not sustainable. Sales managers who lead sales teams must undergo leadership training and understand how to coach for performance since they can impact team performance. What they implement on a daily basis with their teams is far more powerful than a one-time retreat for long-term performance.

Understanding individuals on your team

Knowing your team members is, by far, one of the most important things you can do as a leader to keep motivation "alive" after team-building events.

Paul does a great job of understanding where his team is on the pyramid of needs and helping them move along. He understands that each person on his team is motivated differently and has invested time to understand what "that factor" is and will use it to challenge them to higher performance. At the beginning of the year, not only does he have a discussion with each individual on their sales goals but, more importantly, asks them to consider what personal goals and accomplishments are important to them.

By getting them to tie into their personal growth needs he taps into their intrinsic motivation to achieve their performance goals. One of his team members wanted to save up for an executive MBA program. When Paul learned about this, he made a conscious effort to share information with Janice on the university program and resources. He encouraged Janice to talk with HR and get education assistance. Janice is one of the top performers on her team, not just because she appreciates Paul but because she can see a path for achieving her personal goals, which are becoming a reality.

Bringing motivation "here and now"

Motivation is a continuous process and being able to use current circumstances to improve performance goes a long way instead of relying on big things to drive performance. When Jack has a bad month, Paul knows that only way to get him back on track is to help him develop his self-confidence. He will help him focus on scenarios where he closed a difficult sale and lessons from that which he can apply to the current situation. On occasions, he might have another rep go along with Jack on a big deal.

When Terry closed a big deal, he made it a point to publicly recognize her in front of everyone because he knows that Terry holds herself to high standards and what keeps her going is acknowledgment of her competence.

Paul works with his latest team member, Eliza, on preparing and brainstorming solutions before prospect meetings. He involves his team in solving problems and getting buy-in on initiatives that affect them. He understands that it is not money alone that drives his team. The money comes as a result of the environment he has created for performance. It creates the energy of action over a long period of time. Even when some months are bad, he sticks with his team. He understands that his emotional state affects the emotional climate of the entire team. As part of the program, he is being coached for performance so he can stay above the water and chart the destination when everyone is struggling to keep their heads up. His own motivation comes from teaching his team members to succeed.

Does this come to Paul easily? Absolutely not! It has been a journey and a conscious decision by his company to invest in coaching him to lead his people. Paul's impact to the organization is through his team. That is his primary focus. If he can create the right environment for his team, performance will be on track. The leadership at Paul's company knows that coaching Paul is not a "nice thing to have." It is critical to the performance of his team.

Chapter summary

1. Principals of leading companies understand that coaching is a must-have at all levels of the organization to achieve the highest possible performance.

2. Coaching is a key tool in your sales manager's toolkit that can maximize the effectiveness of each individual team member.

3. Coaching can help sales reps close new accounts more quickly, develop long-term skills that will propel their sales career, and overcome obstacles that hold them back from maximizing performance.

4. Coaching helps people make behavioral change based on their own insights and experiences by encouraging problem-solving.

5. To coach your team, you need to understand what motivates them, and how you can satisfy their five basic needs, in the right order.

6. Don't think money is the only reward people desire. Effective reward systems meet their five basic needs.

7. Motivation is a continuous process, and being able to use current circumstances to improve performance is preferable to relying on big events to drive performance.

8. Leaders that understand how motivation works focus on incorporating it into the daily environment. They understand that while rewards and recognition are important, if the daily work environment does not change to allow people to share ideas freely and have tools to work, long-term performance is not sustainable.

12
The Impact Of Culture On Your Sales Strategy

Coaching is no longer a "nice to have" HR initiative. Rather, its ability to transform your sales leaders and teams becomes the differentiating factor between your sales performance and your competitors. However, coaching for performance cannot exist in a vacuum. It has to be applied in the context of the culture of the organization, which means understanding your culture, its relationship to your sales strategy and the implications it has for your sales strategy is imperative. Without understanding the cultural implications, the effectiveness of any coaching intervention is short-lived.

Marci recently took over as the CEO of her company for the East Africa (EA) region. For the last eight years she has been heading various divisions in locations in

Europe. Marci's objectives for the EA region include aggressive market share growth and increase in sales targets. Strategy formation is one of Marci's biggest strengths as a leader and she has a strong track record of getting results. Like many leaders tasked with building high performance organizations, the culture of her new environment is quickly becoming her Achilles heel.

"I am frustrated with the culture of complacency in the organization, even among my executive team. With strategic objectives we have been given, we need everyone to perform at a higher level. Our sales goals are aggressive. We have to change the way we do things around here and there is resistance to change," she confided.

Marci, like many leaders understands how to use strategy to drive results. With a good strategy there is clarity and a framework for achieving goals and measuring performance. But before she can roll out her sales strategy to the front lines, she has to address the culture at the top. Why is that critical? Culture— our social behavior or norms, the values and beliefs we hold, the unspoken rules about how we do things around here—guides our actions and determines how we fulfill our roles and meet our goals. Unlike strategy, which can be translated directly into action and managed through detailed plans, managing a culture is more complex because we are dealing with unspoken rules and patterns of behaviors, mindsets and assumptions that drive performance. No wonder it's confusing, hard to wrap your head around, and ends up in the realm of HR. They must know how to manage culture since they deal with people all day long.

Both strategy and culture are needed to drive organizational performance and effectiveness.[33] According to Peter Drucker, an organization's culture is a far more powerful force over strategy and determines the success of a strategy's implementation or adoption. "Culture eats strategy for breakfast" is a common phrase that HR professionals will use with you.

Forbes Business journalist Andrew Cave, in his article "Culture Eats Strategy for Breakfast. So What's for Lunch?", shares a study by Mazars, the INSEAD business school on the importance placed on culture. According to Andrew, "The study found that, despite culture being in the top three priorities for company boards, only 20% of 450 London-based directors and board members reported spending the time required to manage and improve it."[34]

The lesson for leaders? Prioritizing strategy over culture is a risk that might not pay off as you drive sales performance.

---

33 Groysberg, B, Lee, J, Price, J and Cheng, Y-J (2018) *"The Leader's Guide to Corporate Culture."* Harvard Business Review.
    www.spencerstuart.com/~/media/pdf%20files/research%20
    and%20insight%20pdfs/the-leaders-guide-to-corporate-culture.pdf
34 Cave, A (2017) "Culture Eats Strategy for Breakfast. So What's for Lunch?" https://forbes.com/sites/andrewcave/2017/11/09/
    culture-eats-strategy-for-breakfast-so-whats-for-lunch/#6fb32a8e7e0f

So what can leaders like Marci do not only to manage the organizational culture but to maneuver through cultural differences, working with a diverse group of people from across the globe?

Culture change is a complex and intricate issue and by no means do I want to oversimplify it. What I would like to share with you are some ideas and tools that I have seen working well to navigate culture issues and pave the way for your strategy to be better accepted and implemented.

Five keys CEOs can use to align culture with strategic initiatives

Key #1: Be willing to acknowledge that culture cannot be ignored

Would you leave out the impact of a change in market conditions to your business when developing your business strategy? My guess is probably not. Just like your business strategy cannot be developed without considering how external factors such as market conditions would affect implementation, it is naïve to assume that the culture you have in place would not need adjustment, or a review at the very least, to be compatible with your strategy. While most business strategies are reviewed over a three- to five-year time frame, the same impetus is rarely given to culture. Acknowledge that culture will have an impact on the success of your strategic objectives. Begin by identifying what environment, behaviors and team dynamics will support your objectives, and which factors will derail your success. By recognizing the hurdles beforehand, you are better positioned to deal with them.

Key #2: Recognize that you have the ability to shape the culture and values of your organization

Teams perform best when they agree on specific goals, have clearly defined roles and can agree on norms. Your team culture, in essence, is a set of norms or rules of engagement that determine how team members work together.

According to Mario Moussa, Madeline Boyer and Derek Newberry, the authors of *Committed Teams*, "Over time the groups' rules change and people begin operating by new rules which conflict with the team's explicit rules in ways they are not aware of. We often misinterpret our own group's rules for collaborating and are blind to ingrained behaviors that actually undermine performance."[35] In other words, it is easy for members of a team to forget the purpose of rules and simply rely on behavior that usually gets them what they want as an individual.

As a leader, you have a strong influence on the culture of your organization. You have the opportunity to

---

35 Moussa, M, Boyer, M and Newberry, D (2016) *Committed Teams: Three Steps to Inspiring Passion and Performance*. Hoboken, NJ: John Wiley & Sons.

consciously and intentionally create these norms or rules on how team members should interact with each other to get work done or solve problems. By modeling the behaviors you want the organization to emulate, you can begin the process of establishing a culture that supports your strategic objectives and brings your team on board. Through your values and actions, you set the tone for how employees interact and operate.

Key #3: Shape group dynamics by creating norms around communication, conflict resolution and decision-making

How do you set clear expectations for team behaviors? What norms are important to shape group dynamics and interaction positively? The authors Mario Moussa, Madeline Boyer and Derek Newberry classify these rules or norms governing how we interact with each other into three critical categories: communicating, deciding and resolving conflicts.[36]

How do we communicate with each other? The author of *The Art of Woo*[37] suggests that we each have a distinctive preference for how we like to receive and convey information. Many years ago, I was working with a robotics company in Atlanta. Their team comprised fifteen PhDs and engineers and the biggest

---

36 Moussa, M, Boyer, M and Newberry, D (2016) *Committed Teams*.
37 Shell, R (2008) *The Art of Woo: Using Persuasion to Sell Your Ideas.*
    Hoboken, NJ: John Wiley & Sons.

challenge was communication. Meetings would stretch for hours or result in emotional outbursts without any resolution. Nobody could agree on a solution and this impacted their ability to deliver on the promise to their customers. One of the first things we did as a team after we looked at the team values was to get everyone to take the DISC personality assessment to better understand their own personality and communication styles.

Once everyone understood their own communication styles in the context of four other personality and communication styles, their perspective expanded. In one of the exercises we grouped people by their personality types and had them share with the other three groups how they liked to give and receive information. Not only did that create "aha moments" for everyone and help them to look at things from a different context, but they also realized their own role in miscommunication. We heard jokes like: "No wonder you kill me with all that detail" and "That's why you tell me all about your weekend before getting to the point."

Being engineers they took it to a whole new level of implementation. They made little tags of the personality types D, I, S and C, and placed them outside each other's cubicles. It was a great visual reminder to adapt your communication style to your recipient. So Dave, who is a high D personality who likes to move fast and get to the point right way, had to pause and consciously remember that he was meeting with

Jonathan, who is a high C, which means he liked details before he could work on what Dave was asking for and not just a high-level context. Instead of jumping right into what Dave wanted, Dave took time to explain the context of the situation, and what would be involved, and took time to answer Jonathan's questions. By being sensitive to each other's styles, the team was better able to understand how to communicate with each other.

Another key rule that they made for themselves as a team when it came to communication about projects was finding a way to give the other team members "WIIFM" ("What's in it for me?") to get them on board with ideas and using data to keep the conversations objective. Anybody leading the meeting would have to come prepared with the WIIFM and facts to share with the team members. By making their own rules around communication they were able to build better relationships as a team.

How about resolving conflicts?

As long as there are teams there will be conflicts. Instead of ignoring these conflicts and pretending they don't exist, decide beforehand as a team how you will handle them. What are your rules to deal with conflict? As you decide on your team's rules of interaction have a discussion around how you will resolve conflicts. A starting point could be focusing on a situation where conflict was handled well and using pointers from those situations to make your rules. In addition, you could also look at "if this happens… then we will do this…" scenarios. Managing conflicts is a skill that takes time but having rules in place is a great start.

How do we make decisions?

Making decisions is a key part of how we function as a team. There is nothing more frustrating than waiting for a peer or boss to make up their minds on something you need to act on now or being part of meetings where no decision gets made. We have all experienced this at times and can't help but misjudge and mistrust each other. During a team charter facilitation with the executive team of an IT company, here are some rules the team decided to create to help them be more inclusive and encourage team members to avoid group think.

1. The leader of the meeting will appoint a "devil's advocate" at the start of the meetings to ensure that we have looked at everything that could go wrong when it comes to important decisions that threaten our business, such as new customer project launch.

2. We will decide beforehand how to come to closure on a decision, whether it is by consensus or by appointing the member best positioned in that expertise to make a decision.

3. The leader of the meeting will be responsible for communicating the decision to everybody (this was important in their case because of the geographical diversity and not everyone may be present at a meeting).

4. Lastly, we will include everyone in the decision who will be affected by that decision (this was important to them so that decisions that impacted salespeople would not be made in the absence of the head of sales).

Instead of focusing on a laundry list of norms, focus on getting a few key norms right. For instance, what are three to five rules that would make your team interactions more effective?

Key #4: Keep these norms alive over time

How do you keep your rules alive? A team charter is a great way to put these rules down in writing and keep it visible in places you most likely meet. But what is a team charter? The team charter clearly defines the direction and purpose of the team and expected outcomes. It not only clarifies goals, roles and responsibilities of team members, but emphasizes expected behaviors, norms or the culture the team wants to create. In teams where the purpose, goals, roles and responsibilities are already well defined, a charter could focus mainly on the norms and culture.

The IT executive team decided to put their team charter in their boardroom and offices. It was a constant visual reminder to actively apply that in their day-to-day dealings. They have also given each other permission to respectfully call them out when they are in contradiction of the rules. This was one of the areas they agreed on beforehand as a team to the what if question, "What if we don't follow this charter and how will we be accountable to ourselves?"

Check in over time if we are still doing what we said we would be doing.

Key #5: Focus on relationships, not stereotypes, in cross-cultural teams

What if your team consists of people from different countries? With a diverse group, the organization's culture is also impacted by perceptions and assumptions about each other's background, and our tendency to stereotype. In my experience, I have found that the only way to get past stereotyping is to make an effort to genuinely understand people and build relationships.

Aligning culture with strategy—how one company did it

As an emotionally intelligent leader, Marci realized that unless her organization's culture supported her strategy, making progress on any objectives was going to be an uphill battle. Like most teams, goals and roles at the company were fairly well defined but clarity around norms needed work. In addition, her executive team also consisted of people from five different countries: the UK, the USA, Kenya, India and France.

Marci understood that unless she deliberately set the norms and expectations that guided her team, it would be hard to get her team to deliver the results she expected. She also took the initiative to build a relationship with each person on her team before expecting everyone's buy-in to her strategic initiatives.

During a team alignment session with Marci's team, we not only looked at establishing the norms around communication, decision-making and conflict resolution, but took it a step further and explored our behavior in relation to these considerations:

- **Communication:** How will we give feedback to each other?

- **Scheduling and timelines:** In the context of deadlines and deliverables—clarifying that deadlines and deliverables were not suggestions but the expectations and commitments we made to each other.

At the end of the team alignment day, the executive team created a team charter to clearly set the direction of the group, with a strong emphasis on expected behaviors and the culture they wanted to see within the team.

Once there was agreement among her senior team members and buy-in from her VP of sales on the goals, the next step for Marci was getting her sales managers and teams on board. Marci knew that two things were critical to her initiatives being success-fully implemented at both the middle and front lines: 1) clear expectations, and 2) for the teams to recognize her support for them. Instead of the usual approach of handing down the strategic initiatives, she focused, along with her VP of sales, on communication to ex-plain not just the strategic initiatives and the new goals, but more importantly, the thinking behind the initiatives, the opportunities she and the VP saw in the market, and what tapping into these opportunities would mean for both the company and the reps.

It didn't stop there. Leading by example is what Marci does best. Before expecting the sales teams to jump on the goals, she knew that she needed to demonstrate the support and resources available to them to enable them to achieve the targets. She also set up regular sales forums where she was able to listen in to what her reps and managers were telling her about the market and their ideas on what would work. One of the roadblocks for quick decisions with clients was the long approval process in place. When Marci found out about this, she and her VP of sales set in place a process for prioritizing sales decisions so reps had the ability to get back to customers within a few hours on major decisions.

For a big deal that the team was working on, she dedicated time to being available to answer any questions around the commercial proposal they had put together and provide any insights around it. She also makes time once a quarter to go on client visits with her VP of sales to keep her pulse on the market. Asked if that is not being too involved, she smiles and shares the example of the president of Coca Cola Europe. "Being Coca Cola, if he can do that, we have no reason to stay locked up in our ivory towers."

By addressing the culture issues head on, engaging the team early on in the process, and leading by example, Marci has raised the bar on performance for her entire team. Her sales team is on target to achieve their goals for the year.

Culture isn't something that can be enforced on people. The best leaders coach their team to create a culture that supports the business strategy. When your culture supports your strategy, coaching for performance creates lasting results.

Chapter summary

1. Culture guides our actions and determines how we fulfill our roles.

2. While you can translate a strategy into direct actions and measure the results, culture is more complex, and cannot be ignored.

3. You need strategy and culture to drive organizational performance.

4. You have the power to shape the culture of your organization by creating norms around communication, conflict resolution and decision-making.

FACTOR FIVE

SALES SCORECARD—MEASURE AND MONITOR RESULTS

13

Build A Reporting Structure Focused On Problem-solving

How do you make your sales reporting work for you?

Regular reporting is a key ingredient of successful sales performance because it keeps the focus on four fundamental questions:

1. Where are we in relation to our goals?

2. Why are we winning sales or losing sales?

3. What problems or trends need to be addressed?

4. What actions should this information lead to/ what should we do differently?

By regularly assessing performance against targets and keeping track of key metrics, adjustments can be made quickly to get on course and capitalize on opportunities. More importantly good sales performance reporting needs to ensure that the goals and information needs at different levels of the organization structure (CEO, senior sales leadership, sales reps and marketing) are met and result in action that moves the organization forward.

Sales reporting at different levels

At the top, reporting that focuses not just on current performance but also on market trends, and regional and product market performance, allows you to see the bigger picture of where the market is moving, to keep your pulse on it, and to tap into opportunities quickly or steer away from situations that will negatively impact the business down the line.

At the middle, management needs visibility on how the sales team is performing and what changes need to be made to get on track with targets. By having visibility on both projected revenues and historical performance, middle managers are also able to present a more objective and balanced view to the senior leadership on how likely the team is to meet the targets. If the team is tracking ahead, it may be time to increase the targets or if the team is trending much lower then perhaps it makes sense to revisit the targets assigned to your reps or increase the resources needed to make those numbers. It might also be an indication of how accurately sales reps might be qualifying new opportunities and the criteria they are using to qualify new opportunities.

Marketing needs to understand how marketing campaigns are performing in terms of lead generation, what channels yield better results and how to drive down lead acquisition cost.

Lastly, from the sales rep's point of view, data keeps the team focused on the objectives and provides clarity on what they need to do to stay on course, especially in an environment that is changing rapidly. An insight into their own past and current performance prevents an overly optimistic outlook on opportunities.

Another way that data can proactively keep sales reps focused and realistic is by giving them visibility on tools, data and reports that focus on the market as a whole and help them hunt in the right places. For instance, if one of your clients is an oil and gas company and you know from market reports that the sector is facing challenges because of dropping oil prices, as a sales rep it stands to reason that you are either going to need more leads in your pipeline as a buffer or not bank your entire commission on those leads.

Align all levels of reporting

Even more important in sales performance reporting is the need for alignment of information at different levels of the organization structure (CEO, senior sales leadership, sales reps and marketing) for solving problems and staying on course to achieve sales targets.

A manufacturing company I work with does a great job at using sales reporting to align the different levels together in solving problems quickly and proactively. They treat their sales reporting with as much precision as they run their machines. Sales reps share their weekly performance results with the sales manager, who in turn shares her team's performance with the sales director. The sales director reviews results from each sales manager responsible for the product line, and has a weekly sales report that tracks performance against goals for the CEO every Monday morning. The weekly reports generate action as follows:

- **Sales reps:** Adjust activity levels to make up for a deficit or re-adjust strategy for getting leads

- **Sales managers:** Take a hands-on role in helping reps close deals and brainstorm ideas or go on a client visit with the rep

- **Sales directors:** Create forecasts, analyze data and compare the previous month's data, observe market trends to anticipate and solve problems before they occur

- **CEO:** The CEO not only gets a report of performance against targets but also a broader sense of the direction sales is headed in, as well as ideas on what needs to be done differently to change course if necessary

By having this mapped out, everyone works in sync and can generate action quickly. Because sales are at the heart of the organization, decisions that impact the closing of sales, such as discounts, negotiation and purchase quantities, can be made quickly. Any client issues are resolved almost instantly because everybody's pulse is on the sale. The regular reporting creates an urgency to take action to respond to client needs.

Why is there reluctance to reporting?

If sales reporting is so useful, why do we dread and almost hate it? Let's start with sales directors and sales reps.

I asked John, one of the reps, what he thought of sales reporting:

"I believe that the reports should be used to solve real-life problems we're dealing with instead of just talking about what needs to be done," he said. "Right now, it just feels like a way to 'police us' and make sure we're doing our job. It doesn't add much value in helping me close sales. I am not sure that senior management even reads it."

Then I proceeded to ask Sally, his sales manager, what value she thought reporting brought to the table:

"I am not sure why we even need this information. It's complicated, time consuming, and quite frankly, I don't believe that it helps us solve anything. More often than not, the same issues are on the report for the longest time without any action."

When asked the same question, here's what the VP of sales said.

"The market is changing so fast and even with all the information it's becoming harder and harder to predict sales. There's pressure on us to watch out for everything that could throw our forecast off. Yes, I realize the pressure it puts on everyone but that's just how it is."

When people don't see the value in reporting and how that is impacting their objectives for the better, it's no wonder it's seen more as a time waster and a bureaucratic exercise meant to control rather than empower employees to meet objectives smarter and faster.

It doesn't have to be that way.

So how do you avoid reporting for reporting's sake and generate information that will trigger action that helps close deals faster, improve negotiation and re-solve customer issues?

Make sales reporting work

Reporting needs to be simple yet meaningful. Most im-portantly the reports, metrics, and criteria you select for measurement should relate directly to the goal and information needed at each level of the organization structure and ultimately result in action that solves a problem. Until an action is taken on the information, reporting becomes an exercise in futility.

I find that there are four steps that go a long way in ensuring that reporting has a positive effect:

Step #1: Start with the end in mind—your information needs should be driven by your objectives

Yes, we can measure everything that needs to be measured, the question is, what action will the information result in? Instead of deciding on what to measure, focus on what the information will help you do.

What information is critical to meeting the business objectives at each level of the organization?

For example, if I am a sales rep, my number one priority is meeting my sales targets. Does the reporting help me manage my sales tasks more efficiently, understand where I might be losing the sale or help me focus on prospects that are profitable so that I can bring in more sales?

That's why data planning is critical—decide what information is needed before you decide on the type of reports needed.

Step #2: Focus on the measures that have the greatest impact or relevance to the objective and what you can control

Ensure that the measures you bring in your reporting are a combination of input measures (what you can influence) and output measures (the end result). For example, the type and quality of activity is an input measure that your sales rep can influence and change, while the sales closed is an output measure.

The reason you want to include input measures is because by controlling and managing these measures you can influence the end results. For instance, if you are measuring conversion rates, and they are low, by coaching and training your sales reps in selling skills, you can directly impact your closure rates and thereby your sales.

Step #3: Explain what the information is going to be used for if you need buy-in

As obvious as it sounds, rarely is the "why behind this report" or "how it's going to be used" shared with people providing the information. As a result, there is no buy-in because people can't see how their activity is relevant to the request and impacts or influences decisions. It's simply seen as another task that management puts on their plate. Informing people about "why" the report is needed will not only create buy-in but also provide you with information you may never have thought to ask for that might actually give you a broader perspective, or a solution that may already exist so you don't have to reinvent the wheel.

Equally important is explaining how the information goes to benefit the providers eventually.

Step #4: Focus on information that solves the problem

The primary purpose of the information you collect is to focus on solving a problem, or at the very least doing something that impacts objectives as a result of collecting that information. If the information is not going to be used, then it might be time to scrap it.

When the focus of the reporting is on problem-solving rather than getting people into trouble, the usual reluctance you hear from sales reps about being micromanaged is rare.

In an instance with a client, one of the sales managers was seeing lower conversion rates on sales for even the best performing reps. As he delved into the issue, he quickly realized that reps were getting similar objections from clients about buying larger quantities for a new tiling product. Prospects needed to see something more tangible than just the brochure before they would commit to it. By figuring out what the issue really was, the sales manager rallied for support from operations and marketing to get product samples for prospects to promote sales. In his monthly sales report, he discussed the cause for the low conversion rate and the action taken.

An important part of the reporting culture at all levels of the organization is the expectation that, once a problem is noticed, action must be taken to solve it within a month.

Regular reporting not only creates momentum and accountability but rather allows problems to be solved in real time and generates better decisions.

By using the sales reporting as a tool to provide resources and help to the sales team, the company keeps reps motivated and engaged. That enthusiasm filters through to the customers and gives the sales reps the confidence they need to make promises to customers they know will be kept. Instilling a sense of urgency both upwards and downwards creates the momentum for action.

What should we measure?

So how do you choose metrics that meet the goals at each level by improving sales performance, optimizing sales activities and building accountability?

Let's start at the top.

Metrics that are valuable to CEOs/senior leadership

The goal of metrics is to ensure revenues are in line with the forecast, and to understand regional and product performance, market trends and opportunities, and threats.

Here are some metrics that are aligned with the goals and needs of CEOs/senior leadership and the importance of tracking them.

Checking the pulse of the business

Metrics and frequency—weekly (W), monthly (M), or quarterly (Q):

- **Average size of transaction/deal**—tracks the type of deals coming through the business and customer buying trends (W/M)

- **Transactions/deals closed**—tracks the total number of deals closed within a given period (W/M)

- **Top 10 deals**—shows the type of customers using the business (M)

- **Sales team conversion rate**—measures how well sales teams are closing deals (M)

- **Number of marketing-qualified leads**—tracks the quantity and quality of leads generated from marketing campaigns (M)

- **Top 10 key accounts**—monitors sales by key accounts (M)

Actions/decisions/questions triggered:

- Are new deals in line with market penetration strategy?

- Are deal sizes skewed too low or too high, exposing the company to risk?

- Among the new deals coming in, are there any observable trends in terms of industries / segments that show an opportunity for expansion?

- If marketing-qualified leads start dropping, does that indicate a change in market conditions, new entrants or slowing revenue growth?

- Investigate any changes in sales team conversion, as these could be indicative of internal issues (eg a change in team make-up) or external factors (eg increased competition / changes in legislation).

- Reviewing key account sales regularly ensures that existing clients are serviced well and any changes in buying patterns are identified and fixed quickly.

Revenue trend metrics

Metrics and frequency—weekly (W), monthly (M), or quarterly (Q):

- **Monthly sales results vs. monthly sales goals—** tracks monthly sales performance, a vital sign of the health of the business (W / M)

- **Annual sales performance vs. annual targets—** measures actual annual sales in relation to annual goals and keeps the focus on the long term (M)

- **Sales run rate—**projects and forecasts annual sales targets based on current sales performance (M / Q)

- **Sales by territory or region**—measures performance by region (M/Q)

- **Sales by product/service line**—measures performance of product/service lines (M/Q)

Actions/decisions/questions triggered:

Dig deeper to understand the causes of variance—internal or external factors.

Internal:

- Is there a change in sales team make-up? Is an intervention needed to turn things around, eg training, coaching, team reassignment, new hires?

- Are internal (eg operational) inefficiencies in the product delivery cycle impacting sales? If so, what corrective measures need to be implemented / recurrent issues need to be solved?

External:

- Get customer and market feedback from managers and reps on changes in buying habits, sales lost to competition and any new trends that are emerging.

- Do any corrective measures need to be taken in the short term to catch up?

- What markets or products are profitable, growing or lagging behind? Where should growth initiatives be focused?

- What measures can be taken to improve underperforming products/markets?

- Identify new opportunties for expansion.

- Craft expansion or penetration strategies and customize solutions that are unique to a particular market instead of a 'one-size-fits-all' approach.

Metrics that are valuable to middle management

From the perspective of marketing and sales middle management, below are some metrics that would be worth considering and details of how they align to the goals and needs of each position.

Sales metrics for marketing directors

Metrics and frequency—weekly (W), monthly (M), or quarterly (Q):

- **Number of leads generated by marketing campaign and channel**—measures total leads generated from different campaigns and channels (W/M)

- **Ratio of MQLs to total leads**—tracks leads that have potential to buy, ie marketing-qualified leads (MQLs) (W/M)

- **Acquistion cost per lead**—tracks the cost of leads generated from each strategy / channel / campaign (W / M—end of campaign)

- **Return on investment (ROI) per campaign**—measures the ROI by marketing campaign (W / M—end of campaign)

- **MQL-to-SQL percentage**—calculates the percentage of MQLs that turn into sales-qualified leads (SQLs), ie a lead that sales qualifies as a potential buyer (W / M)

- **Sales revenue from each campaign**—tracks closed sales by campaign (W / M—end of campaign)

- **Conversion rate**—tracks percentage of MQL leads that convert to sales (M)

Actions/decisions/questions triggered:

- Identify the top marketing strategies and channels that drive the most cost-effective leads.

- Review the quality of leads generated through each strategy.

- Do leads from one source have a higher likelihood of closure versus leads from other avenues?

- ROI data on the performance of campaigns is critical for budget approvals for existing or new campaigns. Look at ROI to determine where to invest your marketing dollars: Where do you get the most bang for your buck, given that different lead generation strategies cost different amounts? Which campaigns need to stop or be redesigned?

- What changes need to be made to ad campaigns or offers to better match buyer personas and generate qualified marketing and sales leads?

- A low MQL-to-SQL percentage may be indicative of misalignment between the buyer personas that marketing and sales view as target prospects. It could also provide insight into the efficiency of the hand-off process for leads between marketing and sales. Identify and agree on the criteria for 'good leads' between the two departments.

- Low conversion rates may indicate poor-quality leads or ineffective follow-up by sales.

Metrics for sales directors/leaders/managers

Lead metrics

Metrics and frequency—weekly (W), monthly (M), or quarterly (Q):

- **Value of your pipeline**—tracks the revenue in your pipeline in relation to your sales goals (W)

- **Sales performance by rep vs. target revenues**—measures actual sales by rep vs. their goal (W/M)

- **Conversion rates by reps**—tracks the individual closing or conversion rates of your sales reps and can be used to calculate the average conversion of your sales team (W/M)

- **Lead aging**—tracks the timeline of the last activity on leads by reps (M/Q)

Actions/decisions/questions triggered:

- Keeping a tab on the opportunities in the pipeline keeps the focus on ensuring consistency in lead generation.

- Involve marketing in lead generation: share insights and feedback on leads received and the outcome of calls with marketing, so campaigns can be adjusted as needed sooner rather than later. Work with your sales team to look for hidden opportunities.

- Find the right intervention strategies for reps to improve conversion rates—eg coaching, team tagging, training etc. Where reps have a better conversion rate than their peers, they can also share their knowledge on what works.

- Are there variations in closing rates between reps? Is this because the sales rep is meeting inappropriate prospects, or is it a skills or follow-up issue?

- Capture issues early on and find solutions. These could involve coaching reps, qualifying deals better, etc.

- Where a lead has stayed too long on a rep's database without any action it might be time to look at your team's follow-up strategy and game plan on "old leads." This could trigger an action to reassign leads. It's also an indication of the performance of your reps.

Conversion metrics

Metrics and frequency—weekly (W), monthly (M), or quarterly (Q):

- **Proposal to sale**—a critical sales metric for managers, as it measures how many proposals turn into sales and has a direct implication on sales conversion rates by rep (M)

- **Number of deals in negotiation**—measures the deals that are at the final stage of negotiation and ready to close (if you're looking at how many deals are going to close this month or quarter, then they should have reached the final negotiation stage in your sales process by now) (W/M)

- **Average sales cycle**—measures the time taken to close a deal (this can be compared with the projected timeline to close) (M/Q)

- **Deals lost**—tracks the number or percentage of deals that are lost during each phase of the sales cycle (an especially useful metric when you have long sales cycles) (W/M)

- **CEO push deals**—measures the number of deals that require involvement on the part of senior management (particularly pertinent when your reps are selling to boards and senior management involvement becomes necessary) (W/M)

Actions/decisions/questions triggered:

- If your proposal-to-sales percentage is low then it may be beneficial to look at the quality of leads your reps are bringing in and the sales reps' skill in closing deals.

- Knowing the number of deals in the final negotiation stage helps project your sales more accurately. It places urgency on identifying actions needed to move the negotiation forward to a close.

- A longer sales cycle can expose inefficiencies in the sales process. Identifying when delays happen, and at what stage in the sales process, can allow you to take quick corrective action so a lead doesn't go cold. For instance, you might have the sales rep approach with another strategy to move forward, take a tag-team approach or create tools to deal with objections. Align your sales process with how buyers wish to buy.

- Being aware of any delays in your sale cycle can help you correct your pipeline projections and prepare a backup plan to increase the leads in your pipeline. For instance, if you take a month longer to close than your original estimate, then you need an extra month's lead in your pipeline to catch up.

- Understanding at what point in your process deals fall through can help prevent this from happening again.

- Identify and involve senior management where needed in CEO push deals, to close deals and give the final push that is needed.

Client retention metrics

Metrics and frequency—weekly (W), monthly (M), or quarterly (Q):

- **Clients lost**—tracks clients who have stopped buying or changed providers (M/Q)

- **Clients who have not bought for six months or more**—most useful for businesses where there are frequent purchases (M/Q)

- **Lifetime value of a client**—tracks the average length a client stays with the company and the revenue earned from the client (M/Q)

Actions/decisions/questions triggered:

- Review client buying habits and reasons for dropping off.

- Identify and solve any open issues that lead to client attrition.

- Increase the number of client visits and interaction to gain a deeper understanding of any changes/trends in the marketplace.

- Initiate marketing strategies focused on client retention.

- Review your referral programs and incorporate strategies that focus on client appreciation and loyalty.

Metrics that are valuable to sales reps

The goal of metrics for sales reps is to help them maintain a full pipeline, track progress and close deals faster.

Remember, you don't want reps taking time away from selling to fill out reports. Whichever CRM you use, it must have the capability of generating a dashboard with key metrics that give you the information you need to make decisions quickly and easily.

Here are some guidelines that you might want to use when designing metrics for sales reps.

Lead generation and closing metrics

Metrics and frequency—weekly (W), monthly (M), or quarterly (Q):

- **Number of new leads generated**—measures if the number of leads will meet sales goals (W/M)

- **Lead source ranking**—helps reps see which of their strategies work best in lead generation (W/M)

- **Percentage of leads progressing in the sales cycle**—tracks which leads move on to the next stage in the cycle (W/M)

- **Number of leads closed**—tracks how many leads each salesperson is closing (W/M)

- **Deal size/value in pipeline**—tracks the average size/value of deals in the pipeline (W/M)

- **Existing client visits**—helps you to maintain a the balance between generating new leads and harnessing existing clients (W/M)

- **Clients who have not bought for six months or more**—most useful for businesses where there are frequent purchases (M/Q)

- **Lead aging**—tracks the age of leads in the pipeline and last contact by sales rep (W/M)

Actions/decisions/questions triggered:

- Review what prospecting methods are working better than others to generate new leads.

- Which industries are showing changes in buying patterns and where may the demand be moving?

- Are deal sizes skewed—ie they rely on a small number of accounts to close and could potentially throw off revenue?

- What actions/support are needed to enable deals to move along the sales pipeline?

- Ensure that leads don't go cold and impact reps' conversion rates.

- Are there opportunities for deal size to be increased? Where should activity be focused to ensure a balanced mix of small and large deals? Are deals profitable?

- What percentage of revenue goal can be derived from existing client relationships? Balance activity levels to service and touch base with existing clients on a consistent basis.

- Develop new follow-up strategies for old leads so that leads don't go cold. Reassign leads if necessary.

Information alone is not enough

These are just some ideas on what kind of metrics to focus on as you drive sales forward. Find the metrics that make most sense for you and are best aligned with the goals you're trying to accomplish. You don't need to measure everything; perhaps you only need to include one or two in each category that show you the direction in which you are headed.

While metrics and reports let you know where you're headed, information alone cannot solve the problems. Metrics or sales reporting for the sake of reporting is a sure-fire recipe for failure. Often the emphasis on metrics vs. the action that needs to take place leaves sales teams demotivated and takes time away from selling. Let your objectives and purpose drive your need for information and sales reporting. Get buy-in for your sales reporting system to succeed or it'll just be seen as one of the things "management forces down our throats."

Chapter summary

1. Regular reporting is a key ingredient of successful sales performance because it keeps the focus on four fundamental questions:

    – Where are we in relation to our goals?

    – Why are we winning sales or losing sales?

    – What problems or trends is need to be addressed?

    – What actions should this information lead to/ what should we do differently?

2. Even more important in sales performance reporting is the need for alignment of information at different levels of the organization structure for solving problems and staying on course to achieve sales targets.

3. Reporting needs to be simple yet meaningful. Most importantly the reports, metrics, and criteria you select for measurement should relate directly to the goal and information needed at each level of the organization structure and ultimately result in action that solves a problem.

4. You can change what you can measure.

5. Select your key metrics from the guidelines and list of metrics that will make a difference to your business.

14
Get The Most Out
Of Your CRM

Google "best CRM solutions" and you will come up with at least 508 products listed as the top 2018 solutions. There is no question that customer relationship management (CRM) is a critical tool to engage with your customers and prospects. It's absolutely essential for monitoring the value of your sales pipeline, understanding your territory coverage and proactively managing your top line. The ability to get insights into your customer and their behaviors is invaluable for creating marketing campaigns, product development and sales activities. Research by Nucleus Research shows that average returns from CRM can equate to $8.71 for every dollar spent.[38] The effectiveness of

---

38   Nucleus Research (2014) "CRM Pays Back $8.81 for Every Dollar Spent." https://nucleusresearch.com/research/single/crm-pays-back-8-71-for-every-dollar-spent

having a CRM system to increase productivity is not up for debate. Then why do 50% of CRM implementations fail even though they come equipped with just about every feature you need to access information, allow sharing of information between departments or minimize loss of information?

Low user adoption is one of the main reasons why even the best CRM with all the bells and whistles will fail. Not just a huge waste of the investment in your CRM but the opportunity cost of not having access to crucial data that can give you an edge over your competition and help you spot opportunities or the amount of time and resources spent by your salespeople in dealing with incorrect prospect data. According to an article published by Harvard Business Review, "IBM's estimate of the yearly cost of poor-quality data, in the US alone, in 2016 is estimated at $3.1 trillion."[39]

So yes, bad data has real costs in terms of money to your business, to both your top line and your bottom line.

How can you maximize the ROI from your CRM and increase the user adoption at your organization?

---

39   Redman, TC (2016) "Bad Data Costs the US $3 Trillion Per Year."
     https://hbr.org/2016/09/bad-data-costs-the-u-s-3-trillion-per-year

Stay true to the purpose of the CRM

Because CRMs can have so many capabilities it is easy to get caught in the trap of wanting to track everything in the system. Soon your CRM becomes an information feeding machine, with your sales reps and users spending more time on data entry than client-facing activities, whether it is revenue generation or client care. So how do you balance the need to track information with adding value to your customers and keeping your users (sales force, marketing and customer service teams) engaged?

Decide on the three most important problems you want your CRM to solve.

For example, if one of the problems you're trying to solve is proactively managing your top line then the data that is entered needs to truly reflect the right opportunities, not just activity. Will the data that your users enter result in solving the problem or will it just be data for data's sake?

During an interview with a prospective client, the sales manager, George, expressed his utter frustration with the directive for reps to log all outgoing calls to prospects into the system. "The calls don't give us any indication of how the month will turn out," he explained.

"The most reliable metric is the first outcome meeting with reps where we can correctly assess the interest level and get a better understanding of budgets. I believe that's what we should be recording to get a good handle on the pipeline. Sales reps spend too much time entering data just to meet their activity levels. It doesn't serve the purpose because it doesn't give our executive team an accurate pipeline projection."

Increased activity doesn't necessarily equal results or impact. Data for the sake of data can lead to frustration for all parties. Decide on what indicators you will track that make most sense for you.

Align the objectives of various stakeholders when buying the system

Monitoring trends, sales forecasting, better access to sales intelligence, cross selling, targeted marketing campaigns, improved products, customer engagement? Each area of the business has a unique need and a specific objective.

I was in a conversation with a potential client who had just implemented a CRM system and was having challenges getting everyone one board. As we started talking, it became evident that Marketing and IT had been given the directive to go ahead and make the decision on the CRM purchase. It was no surprise that they were met with so much resistance from sales and customer service. In all fairness, marketing made a decision based on what they thought was the key objective of the CRM—gathering good market data. While they had consulted with other departments on their goals, they lacked a deeper understanding of how their processes worked, especially the sales process and customer management process and how the CRM would impact them.

Prioritizing one group's objectives over another is a sure shot recipe for failure. As important as it is for marketing to lobby for accurate data for their campaigns, it is equally important for sales to ensure the sales process becomes the foundation for the CRM and for customer service to weigh in on their process.

Engage end users for the CRM to help solve challenges before they occur

Investing in a CRM is a big decision and you certainly can't have your sales team make that decision for you. It is a management decision after all. I get that. But eventually the success of the CRM depends on whether it addresses the needs of all the stakeholders—marketing, operations, management, sales managers and reps.

What can you do about it?

Before you make a final decision on the CRM solution, get input from your sales team, in terms of their specific challenges when it comes to collecting data. Understand the inefficiencies they are dealing with that take time away from selling. Gaining a deeper understanding of their challenges will help identify the right CRM solution. Incorporate multiple perspectives from diverse users so that your CRM solution is holistic and helps each group achieve their business objectives. That way, when you invest in a CRM solution, you can be confident that your system will solve problems at all levels. You've geared the solution to solving problems, not introducing an archaic, complex system that nobody understands and resists because they can't see the big picture.

Address the "what's in it for me" question before and during implementation

"I would like our sales team to show more enthusiasm toward the CRM and embrace the changes. We've put down so much money into it. They should really be using it," said Jeffery, VP of sales.

"Have you talked to them about what's in it for them?" I asked.

"We've told them how it's going to improve the way we do business," Jeffery answered.

Management recognizes the potential of the CRM and the opportunities it provides for the organization, including the sales reps. In most cases, sales reps interpret it as a way for management to monitor their daily activity and perhaps take control of their database. As a result, sales reps view it with suspicion. I have had so many reps tell me they're not comfortable sharing their leads and will often not even input their hottest opportunities into the CRM, or they operate a parallel spreadsheet where they keep their database. They're not clear on the purpose and exactly how the CRM supports them to close sales. Unless the salespeople see how the CRM helps them make money, they're not going to welcome it with open arms. What can you do to get buy-in?

Show them the money. Focus your message on how it will solve their most pressing issues and close sales. Most CRM training focuses on showing reps how to use the software. While that is important, ensure that the managers who are involved with their teams on implementation focus on the primary goal of how to use the CRM to save time and sell. Invest time in training in the software and looking at solving real-life challenges reps are facing, such as keeping track of the next activity, reports that help them look at prospect spending or measuring their conversion rates. Get your vendors to deliver CRM training with the sales reps in mind. Design reports to give sales reps the insights they need. Reports are not just for their managers who want an insight into activity levels or for the CFO and CEO to look at sales forecasts. By helping sales reps make sense of the information that is relevant for them, you open their minds to finding their own solutions and areas of focus.

Your sales process drives your CRM

The best CRM will not make up for an inefficient sales process or business process. Often the CRM solution can be presented as a solution to an inefficient sales process. But that's a Band-Aid approach. Adding a CRM system to a broken sales process will only create complexity for both your customer and the sales reps.

What can you do about it?

Go back to the sales process and assess if it is the most efficient way of serving your customers and replicates the way your customer likes to buy. Breakdown your sales process step by step and how each step leads to the next. Each step in your sales process needs to have a purpose and build the base for the next. Then look at how the CRM can support or add value to each step. For example, can the CRM help your reps log in relevant information on each step, alert them to the next step, etc? Almost all CRMs have the ability to track the sales process. In other words, show how opportunities move along at each stage of the sales process.

If you really want to get a good handle on your pipeline, it is imperative that the CRM tracks and mirrors how your sales reps sell. Each stage of your sales process should show the "value of the opportunity" and the likelihood of closing that sale. Mold the CRM around your sales process instead of making the sales process fit into the CRM.

Prioritize customer experience over information

Jamie's company had recently implemented a CRM system. In the eagerness to track data from all marketing activities and control the marketing-qualified leads, all inbound calls from prospects were directly routed to the marketing assistant before being passed on to sales. That way marketing could ensure that all relevant information was collected, they could accurately qualify the leads based on the selection criteria such as budget, income, etc and check the box to ensure that only qualified leads were passed onto sales.

Seems like a good idea on paper doesn't it?

Here's what really happened. When a call came in the marketing assistant asked all the data collection questions but by then prospects lost interest and often didn't stay on to talk to the salesperson. Why? You already know the answer as a customer. What you're looking for as a prospect is engagement with a company, not an interrogation.

If your first point of contact doesn't handle the inbound calls correctly, that's a leak in your pipeline right there which impacts your conversion rate. To make the process work, my suggestion was either to train the marketing assistant in sales so that she could ask the right questions while engaging the prospect, or to hand it over to sales. Don't let your need for information interfere with the sales experience or customer experience and engagement. There's a reason the CRM has Customer Relationship as part of its description. The ultimate goal of any CRM is to improve the efficacy of your process so that you can serve the customer better.

Align information and reporting needs

If you've understood the objectives of each department and involved end users early on in terms of what they need, that should drive your decision on the type of information you want to collect and process in your CRM. In addition, it is also important to understand how each department wants data to be reported for actionable results. Data planning on the front end will save you a lot of frustration instead of waiting for the CRM to be implemented and then realizing that the reports you want cannot be generated easily or in a format that is useful to you.

What information needs to be collected?

There is also a tendency for the wish list of information to keep growing from "must have" to "would be good to have." Usually the point of data collection falls into the sales reps' laps and the suggestion to them becomes, "When you're talking to clients you should get this information as well."

It seems really efficient. But if you're in sales you know that the purpose of the sales conversation is to engage the prospect, focus on their needs, understand their pain and propose your solution. If your focus as a sales rep shifts to data capture, there is no doubt that the sale will be lost. And even if your sales rep gathers bits and pieces of information that other departments need, they are not going to put prospecting on hold to enter data into the system. You're obviously going to want them to focus on selling.

Before you make a list of all the information that you need reps to collect, ask the following:

- How will this information help us increase revenue or enhance the customer experience?
- What other ways can I capture this information?

Reporting for action

The reports and information each user receives from the CRM should relate to their specific objectives and KPIs, and enable them to use that information easily to improve those measures.

For example, marketing is primarily interested in understanding where the leads come from; sales is interested in understanding buyer patterns, opportunities for upsell and conversion rates. Customer service wants to know how efficiently they are resolving customer issues. A pipeline report that shows how your leads are progressing or where they are stuck in the sales process is important for sales reps to help them move the prospect forward by either providing new information or regenerating interest.

By giving end users the ability to decide on how to collect and report data that helps them achieve their KPIs, not only is each function more engaged when it comes to the hard work of data collection but also creates a sense of empowerment vs. viewing the CRM negatively as a way to monitor and control their activities.

Stuck with a complex CRM? Find another approach

Salespeople hate nothing more than sitting in front of a computer entering data instead of interacting with people and making sales. In fact, one of the most common complaints from sales reps is the amount of time data entry takes. Add to it a complex system and they lose the will to live. No matter how sophisticated your CRM, ensure it is simple and intuitive and can be accessed on the go. Sales reps should be able to have access to it anywhere and anytime if you want them using it. Ease of use in the CRM is the most important factor in adoption.

What can you do about it?

If you've involved the end users' experience in the decision-making process, chances are that you have already addressed the questions and complexities around it. But what if you're stuck with a system you inherited and just have to make it work? This was exactly the situation one of my clients was stuck in.

Rather than forcing sales reps to use the system (the approach had already failed), we had to find a way around it. Instead of pulling teeth with the sales reps to get good data, we hired an intern whose job was to maintain the integrity of the database. Initially there was a lot of opposition from management with comments rife such as "we're giving the sales reps an easy way out." The question is, would you rather see your investment in the CRM go to waste with inaccurate data that means nothing just because sales reps should be doing it, or consider an approach that would improve conversion rates and improve engagement with your customers? After all isn't that the purpose of the CRM anyway?

Just because you're married to a complex CRM, doesn't mean you have to live with compromise and in misery. Get creative and make it work until you have a better solution.

What to look for in a CRM

Whether you are looking to invest in a new CRM or upgrade your existing one, the important point is to keep in mind the objectives above. Here is what I find useful for encouraging adoption from your users, especially sales reps.

Mobile access

You've probably already thought of this but just in case, I can't stress the importance of your team being able to access the CRM on their phones and tablets. If your reps are in the field, they should have everything at their fingertips to respond to customers instead of waiting to reach the office. It's also so much more valuable to enter sales notes right after a sales conversation to stay on top of next steps vs. waiting till the end of the day.

Increase your team's efficiency by linking email conversations to CRM

A really important feature that will save your team, time, duplication of effort and boring data entry. A good proportion of your sales conversations are probably on email. Look for a seamless integration between your CRM and your email system so that when you look up a prospect in your CRM, you can

also see the email communication that has been taking place.

Integrate your CRM with marketing channels

In addition, your CRM should also be able to integrate
with your website and social media accounts. If you're
using social media channels for lead generation,
your CRM should have the ability to track your lead
source so that you're able to optimize your marketing
channels.

Keep it simple and customize the CRM to your needs

CRMs come with an overload of features these days
and less is more when it comes to efficiency. What's
really important is that the CRM aligns to your objectives mentioned above. When you can stick to that,
it's easy to stay away from the temptation of needing
it all. Ask your CRM vendor if features you don't need
can be eliminated. Stick with a simple user interface
so that you're not clicking through multiple windows
and slowing down everything with all the inbuilt
features.

Test before you buy

Don't just pick a CRM because it is popular, even
though your vendor will tell you that each one of

your competitors is using it. Invest in the CRM based on your objectives, that's what determines success. Even better, most vendors have a trial period. Take advantage of that and have your end users test it before you invest time and money in it.

What should I track on my CRM and what kind of reports and dashboards should I be looking at?

The previous chapter on sales reporting demonstrates that once you determine the metrics that are important for you to track, it's easier to figure out what CRM reports will serve you the best.

Here is a quick summary of the important metrics to track in your CRM.

- **Total revenue and revenue by salesperson:** Track your total sales revenue to date in addition to the revenue by salesperson.

- **Value of your pipeline (also called pipeline reports in some CRMs):** This shows you the total value of sales in your pipeline, what stage each lead is at in your pipeline and the probability of winning a deal and potential value of that sale.

- **Source of leads:** Absolutely critical for marketing to understand which channels are more effective in bringing leads and where to invest their marketing dollars.

- **Average length of sales cycle:** Tracks the amount of time it takes to close a sale. Compare this to the timeline you have allocated to each stage in your sales process. Having a benchmark to compare against lets you know if a sale is taking unusually longer and allows you to adapt your sales tactics to win the sale.

- **Sales activity report:** Track sales activities such as calls and appointments by sales rep so that you can help reps to manage their time and be more productive.

- **Deals lost:** As much as you don't want to be focusing on this, the deals lost metric helps you know the sales you lost and understand the reason why that happened so that next time this can be worked on.

- **Conversion rates:** Also known as your win/loss ratio or proposals quoted vs. closed ratio—this is a critical metric as it will let you know where deals fall through the cracks, what the closing ratio is by salesperson. Lower conversion rates can be an indication of how your reps are selling and can help you figure out the best way to work with them to make improvements.

- **Leads report:** Keeps tracks of all the leads you have received, contact information by prospect and how to distribute leads among your reps. In addition, it helps you keep track of the tasks and activities that need to happen to stay on top of these leads.

Chapter summary

1. The effectiveness of having a CRM system to increase productivity is not up for debate. A report by Research Nucleus shows that average returns from CRM can equate to $8.71 for every dollar spent.[40] Ensure your teams are well trained in using the CRM so they get the best value from it and you get the best from them.

2. 50% of CRM implementations fail because of user adoption problems.

3. Prioritizing one group's objectives over another in selecting a CRM is a sure shot recipe for failure. Align the objectives of various stakeholders.

4. To increase user adoption, engage end users of the CRM to help solve challenges before they occur.

5. Mold the CRM around your sales process instead of making the sales process fit into the CRM.

6. Don't let your need for information interfere with the sales experience or customer experience and engagement. There's a reason the CRM has Customer Relationship as part of its description. The ultimate goal of any CRM is to improve the efficiency in your process so that you can serve the customer better.

---

40 https://nucleusresearch.com/research/single/crm-pays-back-8-71-for-every-dollar-spent

7. Address the "What's in it for me?" question before and during implementation. Focus your message on how it will solve your end user's most pressing issues and close sales.

8. Avoid falling for the sunk cost fallacy, if your CRM isn't working, you're holding yourself back. Get creative or get a new system.

Final Thoughts

As you continue on your journey to achieve your sales objectives, following the five essential steps of the Sales Accelerator Model will ensure that you're building a solid structure that will help sales not only today but lay the foundation for consistent long-term sales growth.

When your perspective shifts and expands, it leads to a new understanding of how your sales strategy is interpreted and implemented on the frontline, and it gives you a chance to examine some of the assumptions you have made. A different interpretation leads to different questions. Different conversations start to take place and different solutions emerge as a result of greater alignment from top to bottom. The perspective gaps that plague most companies begin to diminish as you shine the light on the blind spots. Your managers, sales leaders and sales team have a clear and well-communicated strategy, that they know how to deliver on, that is effectively measured and monitored. Being able to manage the emotional climate of your team creates a culture and environment that supports goal attainment.

Having a sales process and marketing strategy that are aligned increases collaboration between the two departments and begins to replace silo mentalities, putting the focus on the customer, where it should be, and solving problems that really matter to the customer.

The right sales leadership in the middle becomes the connector between the top and the frontline, ensuring that expectations are met while creating an environment for peak sales performance. Finding the right people that fit in with your culture and investing in them through training and coaching empowers them to be proactive problem-solvers, step up their game and take more responsibility. When they have access to information and reporting systems that keeps them focused on what matters most, they have the ability to drive sales results.

The five essential steps place sales at the heart of the organization and your customer in the spotlight. Serving your customers, making meaningful connections in the sales journey and creating memorable customer touchpoints, has the power to turn your customers into your biggest sales force that brings in referrals.

In the end, a highly engaged sales team, focused on delivering and communicating value to your customers, will be your competitive advantage in the marketplace.

This is a journey, not a one-off process. You'll need to revisit steps along the way. Some parts will be easier, some more challenging. I wish you luck in your endeavor; I am here to guide you.

I urge you to take your first step right now by visiting www.celebrusstrategies.com. There you'll find the Sales Calculator, which you can use to find out if you're on target to meet your monthly goals. You can also download the Sales Accelerator Assessment, to find out how well you're positioned for sales growth.

Acknowledgments

They say it takes a village to raise a child. My journey in writing this book feels a lot like that. It would be remiss not to recognize all the people who contributed their support, wisdom and time to help me bring this book into the world. I wish to thank my clients and colleagues over the last thirteen years for letting me share their stories, insights and experiences. As much as I thought I was supporting you in the journey, the truth is that the challenges, questions and problems you hired me to solve became a learning opportunity for me and stretched me to think differently. Your nuggets of wisdom, insights, "aha" moments during our sessions allowed us to co-create and design solutions that were better together. I am truly humbled by your trust and faith.

Ken Davidson, Deena Abbott and Roy Davidson, years of working together made me appreciate your perspective as senior leaders and inspired me to get in the trenches with you as you grew the company. I'd like to thank Dr. Femi Oyetunji and Lawrence Nazare, for your leadership and courage to do whatever it takes to create the right culture for performance. Adam Miller, for being the first country CEO in Kenya to take a chance on me as I was establishing my practice here. Nick Langford, for your candidness, open-mindedness and not only entrusting me with your team, but actively encouraging others to work with me.

My mentor and dear friend, Gael Bevan, I am so thankful for your friendship and encouragement, and for always challenging me to think outside the box and acting as my constant sounding board. Rick Crain, thank you for your friendship, support and "tell it like it is" approach. I value that very much. Thanks also to Jodi Mclean at KPI, who got me started on the book and kept encouraging me all the way to the finish line. And to Professor Aditi Bajaj, for bringing your marketing perspective to sales growth and ideas.

Debbie Jenkins, thank you for bringing your reader's perspective to the book and getting me out of my own head. Thanks also to Lucy McCarraher and Joe Gregory at Rethink Press for your advice and support, and to Andrew Priestley for your guidance on my business.

Last, and most importantly, my family. Thank you Mama for sowing the seed early on to become an author someday. Papa, for your genuine interest in this topic and your excellent proofreading abilities. To my husband and best friend, Arif Virani, for always believing in me even when I didn't. My brother Kumaril Pant, for your unwavering support always. My older brother, Rajesh Malik, for being there for me and all of us. My son, Sahil, for keeping me accountable to my word goal every day. My wonderful daughter, Sania, for joining me in the book-writing journey with her own cookery book.

The Author

Yamini Virani works as a trusted advisor to C-level executives of companies with revenues of US$100–300 million in the USA and Africa to achieve sales results. She has helped her clients successfully beat their sales targets in challenging environments. Yamini was accepted into the Forbes Coaches Council based on the depth and diversity of her experience and track record of successfully impacting business growth.

Having worked in over 100 different industries, Yamini understands the challenges and opportunities that exist for businesses, and utilizes her wealth of experience in business growth, sales, and leadership to help leaders reach their full potential. Her extensive "hands-on" experience in solving real-life sales challenges enables her to connect with readers and clients to create a shift in their thinking and find practical solutions that will actually be implemented.

Yamini writes frequently for Forbes, *Young Entrepreneur's Magazine*, *Daily Nation*, and *Business Daily Africa*. She is also a sought-after speaker and has spoken at many leading international conferences.

Find Yamini online at:

- www.celebrusstrategies.com
- www.forbes.com/sites/forbescoachescouncil/people/yaminivirani
- linkedin.com/in/yaminivirani
- twitter.com/yaminivirani

Lightning Source UK Ltd.
Milton Keynes UK
UKHW032248130121
376732UK00004B/353